Not only does lasagne taste good, people love to cook it because it's fairly easy to create and can last for at least two meals. But just because it's simple doesn't mean it's easy. Knowing what ingredients work best can mean the difference between creating rather unexciting fare and an out-of-this world meal.

[Pasta]

The quickest way to get lasagne to the table is to buy and use convenience products, which means you'll probably buy dried lasagne sheets at the grocery store. The best and most reliable choices for dried pastas are brands imported from Italy, which are almost always made with 100 per cent semolina flour. Some of my favourites are Barilla, De Cecco, and Fini.

You have to cook dried lasagne sheets before assembling them into the finished dish. The sheets come in a few styles; the two most popular are flat with curly edges and ribbed with curly edges. I have tested recipes with both and have found that the flat is the best. The sheets help hold the dish together exceptionally well, and if well oiled, the sheets keep fresh for a day or two after being cooked.

[No-Boil Lasagne Sheets]

No-boil lasagne sheets are a modern convenience that eliminates time, pans, and a small amount of your effort in the kitchen. In terms of quality, no-boil lasagne sheets should be made of only 100 per cent semolina and water, just like dried ones.

The trick to achieving success with no-boil lasagne sheets is in the sauce, or, I should say, in the amount of sauce you use in the dish. These sheets tend to absorb extra moisture from the sauce during the baking process. This creates a dish that's dry, rather than luscious, as the sauce reduces down to its heaviest ingredients.

I created the dishes in this book with fresh or dried pasta, but if you want to use no-boil lasagne sheets, simply increase the moisture in the sauces to allow for some absorption. I have found that Barilla offers the best no-boil sheets.

But here's a little secret: You can actually boil no-boil pasta sheets if you want to. The Barilla no-boil sheets have a nice shape—they are flat with straight edges, which makes them an elegant alternative to curly edged sheets. Also, they are smaller in size, so you can create smaller lasagnes. The flat shape allows them to be boiled and cut to fit any pan, which is very convenient if you want to cook for just one or two people.

[Canned Plum Tomatoes]

I find the canned tomato section of supermarkets to be very overwhelming. Generally speaking, most of the options are good-quality products. I have found, though, that for true freshness, the Italian imported labels are the way to go. And if you really want the best-tasting, truly trustworthy products, find an Italian market where the staff actually knows its products. Frankly, I prefer using simple plum tomatoes when making sauce. I usually don't rely on the other ingredients and herbs that some producers add to their tomatoes.

[Olive Oil]

Like wine, olive oil relies on the climate, soil and geography in which it's grown to create its most alluring flavour. Travelling through Italy is a journey through many subclimates, and each location produces its own distinctive style of oil.

Tuscan oils are typically pungent and full-bodied, with a fruity appeal. The Chianti region produces oils of noted peppery flavours. Umbrian oils are creamy, with a fruity taste, and Ligurian oils provide sweet and delicate flavours. Choosing an oil is mostly a matter of taste, and, frankly, it's fun to buy a few bottles, pour some samples into saucers, and get some great Italian bread to dip into each kind. You'll probably find a favourite, and when doing your sampling, be sure to drink lots of wine. You'll be bringing the delicious flavours of Italy right into your home.

Whichever type of oil you prefer, and no matter where it is produced, the finest olive oils are those labelled extra-virgin. Extra-virgin means that the oil was mechanically pressed from premium, top-grade olives without the use of heat or chemicals.

Oils simply labelled "olive oil" have been extracted from the olive using heat or chemicals, then filtered and blended to eliminate much of the olives' flavour. These oils are intended for general cooking purposes where the flavour of the olives isn't that important to the dish. To keep its flavour fresh, store olive oil in dark glass bottles or cans, away from heat and light.

Throughout this book, olive oil is used in many applications. From coating vegetables for grilling to sautéing meats, it is an essential ingredient used for its intense flavours, as in Basic Basil Pesto and Quick Tomato Sauces. Because the need for it varies, I have specified in recipes where you'll need to use extra-virgin oil. While this type of oil can be expensive, it is truly essential to some dishes.

[Sauces]

Sauces are integral to any lasagne. Not only do they lend a layer of texture and flavour to a dish, but they also add moisture for the pasta. In this book, I have identified four sauces basic to Italian cooking, as well as traditional and classic lasagne dishes.

There are as many schools of thought about and "family" traditions for making sauces as there are regions in Italy. While I have made every effort to provide you with traditional, classical sauce recipes, I have given my own flair to them as well.

For example, many Italian kitchens suggest that there is no other way to make tomato sauce than to begin with fresh, ripe tomatoes. Now, I truly believe that the flavours of fresh tomatoes are tremendous—in the interests of time, however, there are so many canned tomato products available today that it doesn't make sense to labour so hard to achieve a similar result. The recipe for Quick Tomato Sauce is packed with the fresh flavours of tomato and sweet basil. I use canned whole, peeled plum tomatoes, crushing them during cooking to extract the most flavour. I have found that the whole, peeled tomatoes go through far less processing than diced and crushed ones, so the freshness that I desire is still intact.

You will find that my Quick Tomato Sauce is exactly that— few ingredients and a quick cooking time allow for a flavourful, intense sauce that is readily available.

[Pesto]

I researched pesto extensively to find what I believed to be the undisputed classical method of preparation. Truly classical pesto should be made in a mortar and pestle, crushing basil leaves— devoid of stems—with salt and garlic to achieve a well-blended, vibrant green paste. Then adding fine cheese, olive oil and pine kernals crushed to a thick consistency. Again, in the interests of time and to save on unneeded kitchen equipment costs, I use the modern convenience of the food processor. For my pesto, the

intense flavour of the best-quality extra-virgin olive oil is paramount to the flavour. The sauce begins in the food processor and is finished by mixing in the cheese by hand. A small amount of butter finalises the sauce with a rich, velvety sheen.

[Pasta Machines]

Pasta-rolling machines can be found in most department stores and specialist kitchen shops everywhere. It is not necessary to have a rolling machine to make fresh lasagne pasta; however, if you are not comfortable with your accuracy with a rolling pin, then a pasta machine will take away the guesswork. With adjustable thickness gauges, the machine will allow you to gradually roll your dough to the desired thickness by simply adjusting the roller. There are also power motors available as an accessory to make it easier to make fresh pasta sheets.

[Choosing a Baking Dish]

If there is a standard lasagne-baking dish, it would have to be a glass 25 x 30 cm pan with 5-cm sides. This size is identified as standard because the traditional shop-bought, dried lasagne sheets fit the 25 × 30-cm dish perfectly. The next most popular are the 20 x 20-cm dishes—the size of your

dish can generally be chosen in regard to how many servings you wish to have. In this book, I have chosen to bake in both sizes of dish to give you the opportunity to use both.

Choosing a dish for baking your lasagne has generally been left up to personal preference. Dishes can vary in material from clear glass (Pyrex) to coloured ceramic, cast iron and enamel. There is not much difference to cooking in glass versus ceramic or metal. What you want to consider is the immediate use of the dish. Will the lasagne be served immediately or will there be a period of storage? Is the lasagne for family consumption or will it be travelling to another location to be enjoyed by others? The answers to these questions will guide you in choosing the correct baking dish. Baking in disposable aluminium foil gives you the flexibility either to serve the dish immediately, refrigerate it for later or freeze it for future use. You may even want to consider using a disposable dish if you are sharing your lasagne with a neighbour or taking it to a party.

The comparison of glass to ceramic indicates no differences other than seeing the sides and layers of the dish, which are visible in a

glass dish. I have not found any difference in baking times or the texture of the end result when comparing them.

One type of baking dish that should be considered is cast iron. Cast-iron baking dishes can be very handy. The baking times will not change, but the end result will tend to be richer, with a crisp crust forming around the edges. In this book, I chose to bake the Mexican Lasagne in a round cast-iron frying pan not only because the round tortillas fit well within the pan, but also because of the cooking characteristics this pan offers. Cast iron imparts to every dish the flavours of previous dishes, because of what is referred to as "seasoning." A well-seasoned pan will not stick and will bake very evenly. Although it's not a common type of baking dish, there are certainly some great advantages to cooking in cast iron.

[Assembling Lasagne]

Lasagne is basically the art of preparing and layering complementary flavours and textures in a casserole fashion, allowing for the flavours to "bake" together, resulting in rich layers of married intensities. Generally, all lasagnes should begin with lasagne sheets on the bottom to create a support, and end with a layer of sauce and cheeses to create a

bubbling, golden top. Everything in between is up to the individual preparing it. Just keep in mind that the lasagne sheets are what bind the dish together. If adequate layers of pasta are used in proportion to the other ingredients, the casserole will maintain its layered configuration when served.

[Storage and Reheating]

Like wine, lasagne improves with age. It's almost as if the word "lasagne" translates to "better the second day." Almost every recipe in this book will improve with overnight refrigeration. This is due in part to a marinating effect. The sauces, pasta and other ingredients have the opportunity to combine and absorb each other's flavours. Many lasagne dishes can be made in advance, covered and refrigerated overnight. One advantage to this is that you can prepare a few dishes over the weekend, then pull them out during the week, heat them covered in the oven at 200°C/Gas Mark 6 for about 20 minutes and serve.

If you want to freeze lasagne before cooking it, simply cover it tightly with clingfilm and foil. Label it, date it and place it in the freezer. When you are ready to serve it, thaw the lasagne in the refrigerator, then bake it as if it were fresh according to the

recipe. Lasagne should last about three months in the freezer, provided that its container has an airtight seal. Use foil baking dishes when freezing lasagne.

When you are freezing previously baked lasagne, I suggest cutting it into individual portions and wrapping them in clingfilm and foil, then labelling and dating them before putting them in the freezer. This allows for small amounts to be reheated at a time. Be sure to allow baked lasagne to cool completely before cutting it to freeze in portions. It is best to cool it covered in the refrigerator. This will firm up the dish so that when you cut it, it will maintain its layered square shape. Individual portions of frozen lasagne should last up to three months in the freezer.

If the frozen lasagne seems a bit dry after thawing and baking, heat up some sauce and serve it alongside.

chapter 2

Classic Lasagne

Here, feather-light lasagne sheets surround rich layers of hearty meat sauce and creamy béchamel, giving way to timeless tradition. Typically, Lasagne Bolognese would be made with homemade "green" or spinach pasta sheets. Either fresh or store-bought pasta can be used. If you have the time and the inclination, I strongly urge you to make the green pasta sheets found on page 122 for a truly classic dish.

[serves 9]

Lasagne **Bolognese**

1L Bolognese Meat Sauce (page 113)

500ml Béchamel Sauce (page 113) made with $1/2$ peeled onion studded with 2 cloves

450g cooked fresh pasta or 450g packaged dry pasta cooked according to package instructions

225g Italian Fontina cheese cut into strips

Preheat oven to 180°C/Gas Mark 4. In an oiled 25 x 30-cm baking dish, place a layer of drained sheets, just barely overlapping. Cover with about one third of the meat sauce and then one third of the Béchamel Sauce. Top with about one quarter of the Fontina cheese strips. Repeat layers two more times. Top with a layer of pasta and the remaining cheese strips. Bake uncovered for 45 minutes or until top is golden and bubbly. Remove from oven and let stand for a few minutes before cutting into squares to serve.

700g lean minced beef

1 onion, chopped

2 sticks celery, chopped

1/2 red pepper, chopped

2 cloves garlic, crushed

1 Tbsp chopped fresh basil

1 tsp dried oregano

1 tsp dried thyme

1 1/2 tsp salt

800g canned diced tomatoes in juice

350g canned tomato purée

12 dry lasagne sheets

2 eggs, beaten

450g ricotta cheese

80g grated Parmesan cheese

2 Tbsp dried parsley

1 tsp salt

450g grated mozzarella cheese

4 Tbsp grated Parmesan cheese

In a frying pan over medium heat, brown the minced beef, onion, celery, red pepper, and garlic; drain the fat. Mix in basil, oregano, thyme, 1 1/2 teaspoons salt, diced tomatoes and tomato purée. Simmer for 30 to 45 minutes, stirring occasionally.

Preheat oven to 190°C/Gas Mark 5. Bring a large pot of lightly salted water to the boil. Add lasagne sheets, and cook for 9 minutes, or until *al dente*; drain. Lay pasta flat on kitchen paper and blot dry.

In a medium bowl, mix together the eggs, ricotta, 2 tablespoons Parmesan cheese, parsley and 1 teaspoon salt.

Oil the bottom and sides of a 20 x 30 cm baking dish. Layer one third of the lasagne sheets in the bottom of the baking dish. Cover with half of the ricotta mixture, half of the mozzarella cheese and one third of the sauce. Repeat. Top with remaining pasta and sauce. Sprinkle the remaining Parmesan cheese over the top.

Bake in the preheated oven for 30 minutes. Let stand for 10 minutes before serving.

[serves 8]

Classic Italian-American Lasagne

When I was growing up, this dish made its way to our dinner table more times than I can even remember. In my house, however, cottage cheese replaced the ricotta cheese (which you can also do, if you want).

12 dried lasagne sheets

FOR MEATBALLS:

900g good-quality lean minced beef

2 cloves fresh garlic, crushed

15g seasoned bread crumbs

30g grated Romano cheese

2 eggs

1/2 tsp salt

1/2 tsp coarse ground black pepper

FOR TOMATO SAUCE:

11/2 kg canned whole peeled plum tomatoes

50g fresh basil

110ml tomato sauce

2 Tbsp seasoning salt

175g canned tomato purée with garlic

1/4 tsp coarse ground black pepper

FOR CHEESE FILLING:

900g ricotta cheese

130g Romano cheese

[serves 8]

Mama Rose's **Meatball** Lasagne

I think the only lasagne recipe that is more traditional than this is Lasagne Bolognese. To find the perfect recipe, I relied on a well-versed Italian to lead me in the right direction. Rose's lasagne recipe has been around for years.

Preheat oven to 200°C/Gas Mark 6. Evenly coat a 25 x 30 cm baking dish with cooking spray or olive oil. In a large pot of boiling, salted water, cook the lasagne sheets to *al dente* for 10 minutes. Drain the sheets and return them to the pot. Fill the pot with cold water and leave sheets until you're ready to use them. Once ready for assembly, remove one sheet at a time, pat it dry and place it in the baking dish.

[For meatballs]
In a large mixing bowl, combine all of the ingredients. Using your hands, crush the ingredients together to achieve a smooth consistency. If needed, add a little cold water. To form the meatballs, moisten your hands with cold water and roll mounds of the mixture (the size of golf balls) together to form balls. Moisten your hands between each meatball to prevent sticking. Place the meatballs on a platter and set aside.

[For tomato sauce]
Combine all ingredients in a medium stockpot. Bring to the boil, stirring to incorporate, reduce heat and allow to simmer while finishing meatball preparation.

Fill a large frying pan with vegetable oil 5cm up the sides. Heat on medium to high heat. Once oil is hot, fry the meatballs until brown on all sides, about 5

minutes. Remove the meatballs from the oil and place on kitchen paper to drain for a minute or two. Add meatballs to tomato sauce and let it cook for 5 minutes.

[For cheese filling]
In a medium mixing bowl, combine cheeses, stirring thoroughly to combine to a creamy consistency.

[To assemble]
Remove the meatballs from the tomato sauce and place in a mixing bowl. Using a fork or potato masher, crush the meatballs into a crumbly consistency and set aside. In your baking dish, begin with 225ml of tomato sauce, layer four lasagne sheets, overlapping each other, over the sauce. Top the sheets with the meatball mixture, then add 225ml of tomato sauce. Top with four more lasagne sheets overlapping each other, then add the ricotta cheese mixture. Layer the remaining lasagne sheets, making sure that they overlap each other. Top with the remaining sauce. Cover the lasagne with foil and bake for 30 minutes until bubbling. Remove from the oven and let rest for 10 minutes before serving.

450g minced beef

1L tomato basil sauce

900g ricotta cheese

225g grated mozzarella cheese, divided

115g grated Parmesan cheese

2 eggs

1 Tbsp fresh parsley, chopped

1 tsp salt

1/4 tsp ground black pepper

12 no-boil lasagne sheets

[serves 8 to 10]

Easiest-Ever Lasagne

No-boil sheets make this version a cinch to make. Lay them crossways in the pan and leave ample space around each one; they will expand as they soak up liquid in the oven. When assembling, completely douse the sheets with sauce or cheese so that they cook properly.

In a large frying pan, cook the meat, breaking it up with a spoon until browned, about 5 minutes. Drain off excess fat. Stir in the sauce and simmer over medium heat for 10 minutes.

Preheat oven to 180°C/Gas Mark 4. In a large bowl, mix the ricotta, half of the mozzarella, three-quarters of the Parmesan cheese, eggs, parsley, salt and pepper.

Spoon a layer of the sauce over the bottom of a 25 x 30-cm baking dish. Arrange three sheets crossways in the dish over the sauce, leaving space around each. Spread one third of the cheese mixture over the pasta. Spoon one quarter of the sauce over the cheese. Repeat the layers of pasta, cheese mixture and sauce to make a total of four layers of pasta. Top the final layer of pasta with the remaining sauce, the remaining mozzarella cheese and Parmesan cheese. Cover with foil and bake for 40 minutes. Remove foil and bake until lightly browned, about 10 additional minutes. Let stand 10 minutes before cutting to serve.

2 Tbsp olive oil

2 whole chicken breasts, boned and cut into 2.5-cm cubes

225g sliced mushrooms

2 cloves garlic, crushed

1 large onion, chopped

1 tsp dried oregano

1 tsp dried basil

1 tsp dried thyme

800g canned Italian crushed tomatoes with basil

450ml tomato sauce

3 Tbsp freshly grated Romano cheese plus 50g

350g grated carrot

1/2 tsp salt

1 tsp coarsely ground black pepper

225g lasagne sheets, cooked *al dente* and drained

6 to 8 slices mozzarella cheese

Preheat oven to 180°C/Gas Mark 4. Evenly coat a 25 x 30-cm baking dish with cooking spray or olive oil. Heat the olive oil in a large frying pan over medium to high heat. Add the chicken, mushrooms, garlic, onion, oregano, basil and thyme. Cook the chicken until it turns white. Stir in the tomatoes, tomato sauce, 3 tablespoons of Romano cheese, carrots, salt and pepper. Cook uncovered for 5 minutes. To assemble, layer three lasagne sheets in the baking dish, top with half of the chicken mixture, 30g of Romano cheese, and half of the mozzarella cheese. Layer three more lasagne sheets and top with the remaining chicken mixture, Romano cheese and mozzarella cheese. Cover and bake for 20 minutes. Remove the cover and continue to bake for a further 10 minutes or until it is bubbly and the cheese is melted. Remove from oven and let rest for 10 minutes before cutting to serve.

[serves 8]

Chicken Lasagne with Mushrooms and Herbs

When I began telling people about this cookbook, the recipes began to pour in. Well, needless to say, they didn't all make the grade, but one that did is this easy, very flavourful chicken dish from my friend Jen.

Courgettes have such a fresh, crisp flavour that it was only natural to incorporate them into a lasagne dish. With this dish, I have breaded and fried the courgettes to intensify their flavours.

[serves 8]

Fried Courgette Lasagne with Spicy Tomato Sauce

Preheat oven to 200°C/Gas Mark 6. Coat a 25 x 30-cm baking dish with cooking spray or olive oil. In a large pot of boiling, salted water, cook the pasta sheets until *al dente*, about 10 minutes. Drain and rinse under cold water and lay on a towel to dry.

In a medium bowl, combine flour, bread crumbs, salt, black pepper and paprika. In a small bowl, combine milk and beaten eggs. Dredge each courgette slice with flour, then dip in milk mixture, then back in flour. Add vegetable oil to a frying pan and fry courgette over medium to high heat for about 4 minutes until golden brown. Remove from the oil and drain on kitchen paper.

[For the mushroom filling]
Using a large frying pan, over medium to high heat, melt

12 lasagne sheets	FOR FRIED COURGETTE:	FOR CHEESE FILLING:	FOR MUSHROOM FILLING:
1L Slow-Simmered Tomato Sauce (page 120) or Quick Tomato Sauce (page 117)	115g flour	700g container cottage cheese	2 Tbsp unsalted butter
	20g seasoned bread crumbs	100g mascarpone cheese	1 Tbsp extra virgin olive oil
2 tomatoes, sliced thin	1 tsp salt	300g Parmigiano-Reggiano cheese, divided	2 medium onions, thinly sliced
	1 tsp coarsely ground black pepper	2 Tbsp fresh basil	3 cloves garlic, crushed
	1 tsp paprika	1/4 tsp coarsely ground black pepper	450g sliced mushrooms
	225ml milk	1/2 tsp salt	1/2 tsp salt
	2 eggs, beaten		1/2 tsp coarsely ground black pepper
	1L vegetable oil		1 Tbsp sesame seeds
	1kg courgette, thinly sliced		1/2 tsp dried thyme

butter and oil. Sauté onions and garlic until translucent, add mushrooms, salt, pepper, sesame seeds and thyme and continue cooking for about 10 minutes until the mushrooms are browned.

[For the cheese filling]
In a medium-sized mixing bowl, combine the cottage cheese, mascarpone, half of the Parmigiano-Reggiano, basil, salt and pepper. Stir well.

[To assemble]
Place 350ml cups of sauce in the bottom of the baking dish. Top with three lasagne sheets, then with half the fried courgette, half the mushroom mixture, then a layer of the sliced tomatoes. Sprinkle with 70g Parmigiano-Reggiano, then top with 350ml more sauce. Layer with three additional sheets, then with three-quarters of the cheese filling. Top with three more sheets, the remaining sauce, the remaining mushroom filling, then a layer of fried courgette and the remaining cheese. Sprinkle with a dusting of Parmigiano-Reggiano. Bake, uncovered, for 30 minutes or until the top layer of cheese is golden brown and the sides are bubbly. Remove from oven and let rest for 10 minutes before cutting to serve.

Polenta is such a versatile food. In this recipe I have prepared it to a rich, creamy texture, flavoured it with Parmesan cheese, and allowed it to cool for use in place of lasagne sheets. The polenta layers, the robust flavour of chorizo, and the delicate nature of the Swiss chard go well together.

[serves 8]

Polenta Lasagne with Chorizo and Swiss Chard

FOR POLENTA:

225ml milk

1 Tbsp unsalted butter

1/2 tsp salt

1 tsp sugar

150g stone-ground yellow cornmeal

50g grated Parmesan cheese

FOR THE FILLING:

4 Tbsp unsalted butter

4 Tbsp olive oil

1 medium onion, finely chopped

1 carrot, peeled and finely chopped

1 celery stick, finely chopped

2 cloves garlic, chopped

225g chorizo chopped sausage to 5mm dice

115ml dry red wine

400g canned diced tomatoes with purée

salt and freshly ground black pepper

1/4 tsp red pepper flakes

1 bunch (about 450g) Swiss chard, washed, patted dry and roughly chopped

50g crumbled feta cheese

1/2 tsp freshly ground nutmeg

1/4 tsp ground ginger

2 cloves garlic, crushed

3 Tbsp fresh basil, shredded

1 tsp fresh Italian parsley, shredded

120ml double cream

225g fresh mozzarella cheese, sliced

[For polenta]

Combine milk, butter, salt and sugar in a heavy-bottomed saucepan (a Teflon-coated one works best). Bring to a simmer, just until steaming. Add cornmeal in a steady stream, whisking continuously to combine it and prevent lumps from forming. Once combined, reduce the heat to a simmer and continue to cook, stirring continuously, until the mixture is thick and begins to pull away from the sides of the pot, about 2 to 5 minutes. Remove from the heat and add the Parmesan cheese. Combine thoroughly.

Oil a Swiss roll baking tray. Pour the polenta into it, spreading it flat with an oiled spatula. Cool until firm, about 1 hour. (The polenta can be made up to a day ahead. Cover with clingfilm and refrigerate.)

[For sausage mixture]

In a large saucepan over medium heat, melt 2 tablespoons of butter with 2 tablespoons of olive oil. Add the onion, carrot and celery, and cook, stirring, until tender but not browned, about 10 minutes. Stir in the garlic. Add the sausage and cook, stirring, until browned, about 10 minutes. Add the wine and cook until the liquid evaporates, about 2 additional minutes. Add the tomatoes and their juice, the parsley and the red pepper flakes. Stir to combine. Season with salt and pepper, and reduce the heat to a simmer. Simmer uncovered until the mixture is thickened, about 30 minutes.

[For Swiss chard purée]

In a medium saucepan, heat the remaining 2 tablespoons of butter with the remaining 2 tablespoons of olive oil. Add the Swiss chard, tossing it to coat it with oil. Cover and let steam until the chard is tender and bright green in colour, about 5 minutes. Stir occasionally to ensure that the chard is tender. Remove the saucepan from the heat and set it aside. Preheat the oven to 200°C/Gas Mark 6. Oil a 20 x 30-cm baking dish. In a food processor, combine the chard, feta cheese, nutmeg, ginger, garlic, basil and parsley. Process the mixture until puréed. Add the cream, scrape down the sides and process the mixture until it is well combined and creamy.

[To assemble]

Remove the polenta from the refrigerator. Cut the polenta into twelve equal squares. Arrange half of the squares in the bottom of the baking dish. Spoon on half of the Swiss chard purée, coating the polenta evenly. Top the purée with half of the sausage mixture. Top the sausage with half of the fresh mozzarella cheese slices. Repeat the layers using the remaining ingredients. Bake until the cheese melts and the sauce is bubbling, about 30 minutes. Let stand for 5 minutes before serving. Serve hot, directly from the oven.

2 Tbsp vegetable or olive oil

450g dry or fresh lasagne sheets

500ml Slow-Simmered Tomato
Sauce (page 120), Quick Tomato
Sauce (page 117), or 800ml
spaghetti sauce

900g ricotta or cottage cheese

225g grated mozzarella cheese

225g crumbled feta cheese

150g grated Parmesan cheese

[serves 9]

Four-Cheese Lasagne

Let the combination of cheeses in this dish do all the
work. The most difficult part of this dish is selecting
a sauce. The Slow-Simmered Tomato Sauce will
give it a deep, rich flavour whereas the Quick Tomato
Sauce will impart a more fresh, spring-like taste.
Whatever your decision, the cheeses will pair
perfectly and the flavours will be simple but elegant.

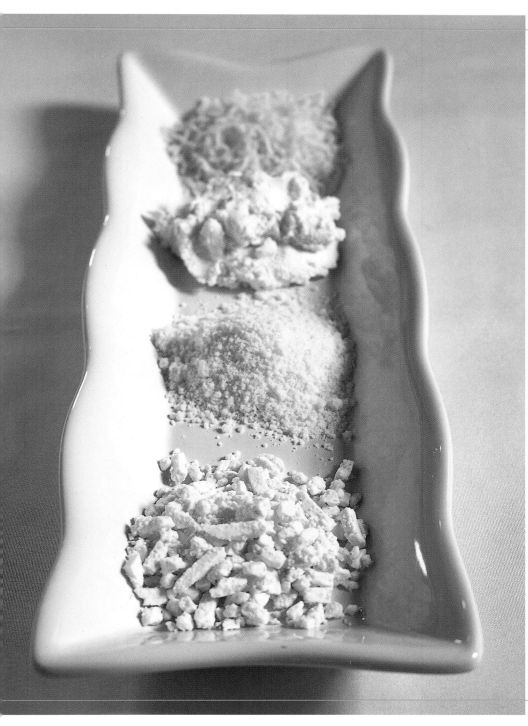

Preheat oven to 190°C/Gas Mark 5. Oil the sides and bottom of a 25 x 30-cm baking dish. Bring a large pot of lightly salted water the a boil. Add dried pasta and cook for 8 to 10 minutes, or until *al dente*. If using fresh pasta, cook for only 2 to 4 minutes.

In a blender or with an electric mixer, blend the tomato sauce and ricotta cheese together until smooth. In a small bowl, combine the basil and parsley. Spoon a little of the sauce mixture into the bottom of the baking dish. Place a layer of cooked pasta over the sauce, and sprinkle a portion of the mozzarella, feta, Parmesan and herbs over the pasta. Repeat the layering of sauce, pasta, cheeses and herbs, finishing with a cheese layer sprinkled with remaining herbs.

Bake in the preheated oven for 30 to 45 minutes until the cheese is bubbly and golden. Remove from the oven and let rest for 10 minutes before slicing to serve.

Lasagna

12 dry lasagne sheets

225g ricotta cheese

100g goat's cheese

225g Fontina cheese, grated

225g mozzarella cheese, grated

1 recipe Basic Basil Pesto
(page 118)

175g roasted red peppers,
drained and thinly sliced

175g roasted yellow peppers,
drained and thinly sliced

[serves 4 to 6]

Pesto Lasagne **with Roasted Red and Yellow Peppers**

This is a great version of the traditional Lasagne con Pesto from the Ligurian region of Italy. A bright summer day and a silky glass of Pinot Grigio are the best accompaniments for this dish.

Preheat oven to 190°C/Gas Mark 5. Oil bottom and sides of an 20 x 20-cm baking dish. Bring a large pot of salted water to the boil. Boil pasta sheets for 10 minutes until *al dente*.

In a small bowl, combine the ricotta and goat's cheeses, and blend well. In another small bowl, combine the Fontina and mozzarella cheeses. Line the bottom of the baking dish with three sheets of pasta, and top with one third of the pesto topping and one third of the Fontina cheese mixture. Add another layer of three pasta sheets.

Top with half of the ricotta cheese mixture and then with two thirds of the roasted red and yellow peppers, followed by one third of the Fontina cheese mixture. Then add three more sheets of pasta. Repeat with a layer of pesto, then the remaining Fontina cheese mixture, three pasta sheets, ricotta cheese mixture, roasted peppers and the pesto as the last layer.

Bake for 30 minutes until it is bubbly and the pesto begins to darken around the edges. Remove from oven and let rest 10 minutes before cutting to serve. For an easier, thinner dish, omit the ricotta cheese mixture from the layers. The result is less rich and a bit oilier, but still tastes terrific.

Pre-heat oven to 200°C/Gas Mark 6. Cook lasagne sheets according to package directions. Drain them and lay them flat on a towel to dry. In a large frying pan over medium heat, sauté the onion, mushrooms and garlic in oil until they are tender and the mushrooms begin to give off their juices and darken. Place the onion and mushroom mixture in a mixing bowl and add the cream cheese. Gradually stir in the cottage cheese, mozzarella cheese, egg, basil, salt and pepper. Chop the prawns and crab and add to the mixture; combine well. In another mixing bowl, combine the mushroom soup, milk and wine. Oil a 25 x 30-cm baking dish and coat the bottom with half of the mushroom mixture. To assemble roulades, lay the lasagne sheets flat on a large work surface, and spread the seafood mixture evenly over the lasagne sheets, staying close to the edge of the pasta. Begin at one end and roll the pasta up into a cylinder. Place it seam-side down in the baking dish. Repeat with remainder of the sheets and filling. Top roulades with remainder of mushroom sauce, and top with Parmesan cheese. Bake for 20 to 30 minutes until the tops are bubbling and begin to brown. Remove roulades from oven and let them rest for 5 minutes before serving. Serve two roulades per person, garnishing them with fresh basil leaves and sauce from the bottom of the baking dish.

[serves 6]

Seafood Lasagne **Roulades**

This is a tremendous dish with intense flavours and a very elegant presentation. The roulades are such a simple way to use lasagne sheets, with beautiful results. Serve these with fresh steamed or roasted asparagus spears. Best of all, they are so easy to prepare, taking very little time to pull together for an intimate dinner.

12 lasagne sheets

2 Tbsp olive oil

2 medium onions, chopped

90g shiitake mushrooms, rinsed clean and dried, finely chopped

1 clove garlic, crushed

225g cream cheese

350g cottage cheese

50g mozzarella cheese, grated

1 egg

1 Tbsp chopped fresh basil or 2 tsp dried

salt and pepper

450g boiled baby prawns

225g crabmeat, cleaned

500ml condensed mushroom soup

75ml milk

75ml dry white wine

50g grated Parmesan cheese

Fresh basil leaves for garnish

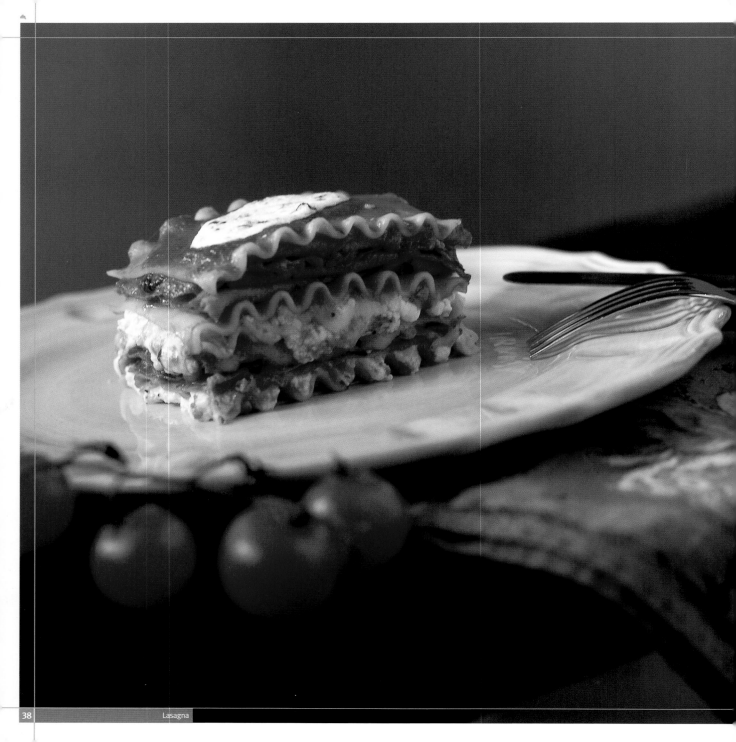

Lasagna

450g ricotta cheese

3 tbsp fresh basil, chopped

1 Tbsp dried oregano

2 eggs

1/8 tsp red pepper flakes

50g grated Parmesan cheese

450g dried or fresh lasagne sheets

500ml Quick Tomato Sauce
(page 117)

225g prosciutto, thinly sliced

225g Genoa salami, thinly sliced

225g smoked deli ham, thinly sliced

225g sweet capicola, thinly sliced

225g provolone cheese, thinly sliced

225g grated mozzarella cheese

Preheat oven to 190°C/Gas Mark 5. Coat the bottom and sides of a 25 x 30-cm baking dish evenly with olive oil. In a large mixing bowl, combine ricotta cheese, basil, oregano, eggs, pepper flakes and Parmesan cheese. Mix until eggs are thoroughly combined.

In a large pot of salted, boiling water, cook the dried pasta according to package directions; cook fresh pasta for 2 minutes. Drain the pasta and rinse it with cold water. Place it on kitchen paper to dry before using it in the dish.

Place 100ml cup tomato sauce on the bottom of the baking dish. Top with a layer of lasagne sheets. Top sheets with 75g of the ricotta cheese mixture, spreading evenly over the pasta. Top with another layer of pasta. Top pasta with half of the meats, layering them evenly. Top the meat with half of the provolone, and top this with half of the shredded mozzarella cheese. Repeat with a layer of pasta, then 150ml of sauce, then 75g ricotta cheese mixture. Top the ricotta cheese mixture with another layer of pasta, then the remainder of the meats, provolone cheese and mozzarella cheese. Finish with a final layer of pasta, topped with the remainder of the tomato sauce and the remaining ricotta cheese mixture.

Coat a large sheet of foil with oil and cover the baking dish with it, oil-side down. Bake for 30 minutes, covered. Remove foil and bake for an additional 15 to 20 minutes or until the top is bubbly and the cheese begins to brown. Remove the lasagne from the oven and let it rest for 10 minutes before cutting to serve.

[serves 9]

Italian Grinder Lasagne

Sitting in a little Italian pizzeria one day,
I ordered the meaty stuffed pizza. One bite into
it and I thought, "This has to be a lasagne."
I love the dense texture of this dish—I believe
you will, too.

chapter 3

Lasagne **Around the World**

9 dried lasagne sheets

1 Tbsp butter

2 Tbsp extra-virgin olive oil

1 small onion, chopped

3 cloves garlic, crushed

1 small green pepper, chopped

1 small red pepper, chopped

450g skinless, boneless chicken breasts, cooked and diced

1/2 tsp cayenne pepper

2 Tbsp cider vinegar

2 Tbsp Worcestershire sauce

1 Tbsp Thai curry paste, optional

1L Quick Tomato Sauce (page 117) or Slow-Simmered Tomato Sauce (page 120)

350ml water

3 Tbsp hot sauce

1 egg, beaten

400g ricotta cheese

225g grated mozzarella cheese

75g crumbled blue or Gorgonzola cheese

Preheat oven to 180°C/Gas Mark 4. Evenly coat a 25 x 30-cm baking dish with cooking spray or olive oil. In a large pot of boiling, salted water, cook the lasagne sheets until *al dente*, about 10 minutes. Drain and rinse under cold water, and set aside on a towel to dry.

[For chicken mixture]
In a large frying pan over medium to high heat, melt the butter and oil. Sauté the onion, garlic and peppers until tender and onions become translucent, about 5 minutes. Add chicken and cayenne pepper, stir and cook for an additional 2 minutes. Add vinegar, Worcestershire sauce and Thai curry paste, stir and continue to cook for another minute. Add tomato sauce and water, bring to the boil for 1 minute, add hot sauce, reduce heat, and allow to cook for 10 more minutes. Remove from heat and set aside. In a medium mixing bowl, combine the beaten egg with the ricotta cheese and set aside.

[To assemble]
Layer the bottom of the baking dish with three lasagne sheets, top with 400g of the chicken mixture and half of the ricotta cheese mixture, and sprinkle with half of the mozzarella cheese. Top with three more pasta sheets and repeat with 400g chicken mixture, remaining ricotta cheese, and remaining mozzarella cheese. Top with one last layer of lasagne sheets and remaining chicken mixture. Cover dish and bake for 30 minutes. Remove cover, sprinkle crumbled blue cheese on top, and bake an additional 10 minutes until top is golden and bubbly. Remove from oven and let rest for 10 minutes before cutting to serve.

[serves 8]

Buffalo Chicken Lasagne

You can eat this buffalo chicken with a fork rather than your hands and still have all the great, spicy flavours of your favourite hot wings. If you want, dip some fresh celery sticks into the sauce.

1 ½ kg of aubergines, peeled, sliced 1cm thick

4 Tbsp olive oil

900g minced lamb

2 Tbsp olive oil, extra

2 large onions, chopped

75g grated carrot

50g chopped leeks

3 cloves garlic, finely chopped

1 ½ kg canned peeled, diced tomatoes

2 Tbsp tomato purée

100ml red wine

225ml beef stock

1 Tbsp dried oregano

2 sprigs fresh thyme

1 tsp paprika

2 bay leaves

4 Tbsp chopped fresh Italian parsley

1 tsp ground cumin

2 tsp dried basil

1 tsp ground cinnamon

1 Tbsp chopped fresh mint, optional

Pinch ground cloves

Salt and coarsely ground black pepper

700ml Béchamel Sauce (page 113)

¼ tsp nutmeg

225g feta cheese plus 50g

Cream or milk as needed

¼ cup fine, dried bread crumbs

¼ cup freshly grated Parmesan cheese

9 lasagne sheets, dried or fresh

[serves 9]

Greek-Style Lamb and Aubergine Lasagne

Sometimes referred to as *moussaka,* rich meat sauce using lamb with herbs and spices is a Greek tradition. Both lamb and aubergine are popular in Greek cuisine, but they are also tremendously appreciated in Italian kitchens.

Preheat oven to 200°C/Gas Mark 6.

[To prepare aubergine]
Peel and cut into slices 1cm thick. Place aubergine slices in a colander, sprinkle them with salt and let them stand for 1 hour to drain off juices. Rinse the aubergine in cold water and pat dry. Coat both sides of sliced aubergine generously with extra-virgin olive oil. Place the aubergine on a baking sheet in the oven, and bake for 15 to 20 minutes, turning once until both sides are browned. Transfer to kitchen paper to drain.

[To prepare meat sauce]
In a large stockpot or saucepan, heat the oil over medium to high heat. Brown the lamb, about 10 minutes, breaking it up into small chunks as it cooks. Add the onion, carrot and leeks. Cook until tender, about 15 minutes. Add the garlic, tomatoes and tomato purée. Cook for an additional 2 minutes, stirring to combine. Add the red wine, beef stock and herbs. Reduce the heat and simmer for about 30 minutes. The recipe makes more meat sauce than is necessary for this dish. Serve the extra alongside the lasagne slices.

Meanwhile, in a medium saucepan over medium heat, heat the Béchamel Sauce with the nutmeg and feta cheese. Heat through, melting the feta. Add cream or milk, a little at a time, if the sauce appears to be too thick to pour.

[To assemble]

Coat a 25 x 30-cm baking dish evenly with cooking spray or olive oil. Place three pasta sheets in the bottom, and top with an even layer of half of the aubergine, then about 500ml of meat sauce and half of the Béchamel Sauce. Sprinkle with Parmesan cheese. Add another layer of pasta sheets, topping with the remainder of the aubergine and 500ml of meat sauce. Top with the remaining three pasta sheets, then with the remaining Béchamel. Sprinkle the top with bread crumbs and 50g crumbled feta cheese. Place in the oven and bake for 30 minutes or until golden and bubbly. Remove from the oven and let rest for 10 minutes before cutting to serve.

2 Tbsp extra-virgin olive oil

1 large onion, finely chopped

75g prosciutto di Parma,
finely chopped

4 Tbsp Italian parsley,
finely chopped

2 Tbsp chopped shallots

450g assorted wild and exotic
mushrooms (oyster, shiitake,
lobster, cremini, etc.)

500ml beef stock

2 Tbsp garlic, crushed

3 Tbsp fresh basil, chopped

1 Tbsp fresh oregano, chopped

150ml dry white wine

800g plus 400g canned crushed
tomatoes

1/4 tsp paprika

1/4 tsp cayenne pepper

salt and pepper

300g plus 2 Tbsp grated
Parmigiano-Reggiano cheese

115g grated mozzarella cheese
plus 50g

120ml double cream

50ml milk

450g dried pasta sheets cooked
according to package directions
or 450g fresh pasta blanched
for 2 minutes and drained

Preheat the oven to 180°C/Gas Mark 4. Lightly oil a 25 × 30-cm baking dish.

In a large sauté pan, heat the olive oil. When the oil is hot, sauté the onions and prosciutto for about 3 minutes or until the onions are wilted and begin to caramelise.

Add 50g of minced parsley, shallots and mushrooms. Combine and sauté them for about 5 minutes or until the mushrooms begin to brown and soften. Add 500ml of beef stock, stirring vigorously to deglaze the pan—continue to cook for an additional 45 minutes to concentrate the flavours. Season with salt and pepper. Stir in the garlic, basil and oregano. Cook for an additional 3 minutes to combine the flavours. Remove the mixture from the heat. Strain the mushroom mixture, reserving the liquid.

Pour the liquid back into the sauté pan. Heat and stir vigorously to remove any particles along the sides of the pan. Add the wine and continue to deglaze the pan. Continue to cook the liquid until a glaze is formed, stirring occasionally. Add the tomatoes, paprika, and cayenne, and combine thoroughly. Continue to cook for 20 minutes, stirring occasionally. Season with salt and pepper. Add the mushroom mixture to the sauce. Combine and remove the sauce from the heat.

[To assemble]
Spoon a small amount of the sauce on the bottom of the baking dish, covering evenly. Layer pasta sheets over the sauce, being careful not to overlap them. Cut the pasta sheets to fit the baking dish if necessary. Repeat with a thick layer of mushroom sauce. Sprinkle with Parmesan cheese and a generous amount of mozzarella cheese. Top with three additional sheets of pasta and repeat with remaining mushroom sauce, Parmesan cheese, mozzarella cheese and pasta sheets. Ensure that the last layer in the baking dish is the pasta sheets. Mix the double cream with the milk, 2 tablespoons Parmigiano-Reggiano cheese, and 50g mozzarella cheese. Season with salt and pepper. Pour over the top of the lasagne. Cover the lasagne with foil and bake for 30 minutes. Remove the cover and bake for an additional 15 to 20 minutes or until the top layer of cheese becomes brown and bubbly. Remove from oven. Allow to rest for 10 minutes before cutting to serve. If there is any remaining mushroom sauce, serve alongside the lasagne.

[serves 9]

Robust Tomato and Wild Mushroom Lasagne

Tomatoes and wild mushrooms come together in this hearty, wildly flavourful lasagne. With a bite of cayenne, the mushrooms add extra layers of rich, intense flavours throughout the dish.

Preheat oven to 180°C/Gas Mark 4. Evenly coat the sides and bottom of a 25 × 30-cm baking dish with cooking spray or olive oil. In a large pot of boiling, salted water, cook the pasta until *al dente*—10 minutes for dry pasta, 2 to 3 minutes for fresh. Remove from hot water and run under cold water. Set aside on a towel to dry.

In a small mixing bowl, combine 3 eggs, garlic powder, onion powder, 150g Parmesan cheese, Italian seasoning, cayenne pepper, salt, and black pepper. In a separate shallow dish, combine the flour with the bread crumbs.

Heat oil in a large frying pan. Dredge aubergine slices in flour, then in egg mixture, and then in flour again. Fry slices in preheated oil, two to three slices at a time, until browned on both sides, about 2 to 3 minutes per side. Remove slices from oil and place on kitchen paper to drain. Continue until all slices are fried.

In a large bowl, combine ricotta cheese, 75g mozzarella cheese, remaining Parmesan cheese, parsley, basil, remaining egg, and spinach, and mix well.

[To assemble]
Layer one third of the tomato sauce in the bottom of the baking dish, then three lasagne sheets, half the aubergine slices, half the tomato slices, three additional lasagne sheets, ricotta cheese mixture, three more lasagne sheets, one third of the sauce, remaining aubergine, then repeat with the tomato slices, lasagne sheets, and tomato sauce, and top with remaining mozzarella cheese. Cover with foil coated with cooking spray, bake for 20 minutes, remove foil, and continue to bake for an additional 15 minutes until cheese is browned and bubbly. Remove from oven and let rest for 10 minutes before cutting to serve.

[serves 8]

Aubergine and Tomato
Lasagne **Gratin**

Two Italian staples, aubergine and tomato, blend together to melt into a flavourful dish rich in Italian tradition. This lasagne combines breaded and fried aubergine with juicy vine-fresh tomatoes to create a layered gratin.

12 lasagne sheets, dried or fresh

4 eggs

1 tbsp garlic powder

1 tsp onion powder, optional

300g grated Parmesan cheese, divided

1 Tbsp Italian seasoning

1/2 tsp cayenne pepper

1/2 tsp salt

1/2 tsp coarse ground black pepper

115g flour

15g seasoned bread crumbs

500ml vegetable oil for frying

2 large aubergines, peeled and cut into 5mm slices

400g ricotta cheese

115g grated mozzarella cheese

2 Tbsp fresh Italian parsley, chopped

2 Tbsp fresh basil, chopped

300g frozen chopped spinach, thawed, drained, and pressed dry

700 ml Quick Tomato Sauce (page 117) or Slow-Simmered Tomato Sauce (page 120)

4 vine-ripened tomatoes, sliced 5mm thick, seasoned with salt and black pepper

Lasagna

two (225g) chicken breasts, cooked and cut into chunks

2 Tbsp olive oil

75g chopped onion

75g chopped red pepper

50g frozen sweet corn, thawed

2 cloves garlic, chopped

1½ tsp ground cumin

1 tsp chilli powder

450g canned black beans, rinsed and drained

450g canned refried black beans

500ml canned tomato sauce

100ml salsa

300ml canned enchilada sauce

2 Tbsp chopped fresh coriander plus 2 Tbsp for garnishing

9 corn tortillas

225g grated cheddar cheese

175g grated Monterey Jack cheese

75g sliced black olives (optional)

50ml soured cream for garnish

8 sprigs fresh coriander for garnish

Preheat oven to 180°C/Gas Mark 4. Spray the sides and bottom of a 25 × 30-cm baking dish with cooking spray. In a medium saucepan, bring sufficient water to the boil to cook the chicken. Boil the chicken for about 10 minutes until cooked through.

Remove from water and set aside to cool. Once it is cool to the touch, chop the chicken into small chunks. In a large frying pan on medium-high heat, heat the olive oil. Add the onion, pepper, corn and garlic. Sauté the vegetables until they are wilted and translucent, about 10 minutes. Add the cumin and chilli powder. Continue to cook for an additional 2 minutes. Add the black beans and chicken. Stir to incorporate flavours and heat through.

Remove the mixture from the heat and set aside. Place a medium-sized saucepan on medium heat and add the refried beans, tomato sauce, salsa, enchilada sauce and fresh coriander. Heat to boiling and remove from the heat.

[To assemble]
Place one third of the tomato sauce mixture on the bottom of the baking dish; cover with three tortillas. Top the tortillas with half of the chicken mixture then another one third of the sauce, topping this with half of the Cheddar cheese. Repeat the layers with three tortillas, the remaining chicken mixture, sauce, and Cheddar cheese, then top all this with three more tortillas, monterey jack cheese, and sliced black olives. Place in the oven uncovered, and bake for 20 to 30 minutes until the top is browned and bubbly. Remove from oven and let rest for 10 minutes before cutting to serve. To serve, place the lasagne on a plate, put a tablespoon of soured cream on top and garnish with a sprig of coriander.

[serves 8]

Mexican Black Bean Lasagne

Replacing lasagne sheets with tender corn tortillas gives a Southwestern twist to an Italian classic. The use of black beans keeps down the calories, while fresh vegetables and spices impart great flavours. Olé!

Straight from New Orleans, this intensely flavoured dish, topped with a unique cornbread crust, is easy to make and delicious. I have combined cayenne pepper, chilli paste and hot pepper sauce with garden-fresh vegetables to create this truly Creole experience. The cornbread topping browns to a dense, moist crust.

[serves 9]

Bourbon Street Lasagne with Cornbread Crust

9 sheets fresh or dry lasagne
pasta

6 Tbsp vegetable or olive oil

2 sticks celery, chopped

1 green pepper, chopped

1 red pepper, chopped

1/2 onion, chopped

100g frozen sweetcorn, thawed

450g fresh okra, sliced

1 1/2 Tbsp fresh thyme leaves,
chopped, or 2 1/2 tsp dried

1 1/2 Tbsp fresh sage leaves,
chopped, or 2 1/2 tsp dried

1 1/2 Tbsp fresh rosemary,
chopped, or 2 1/2 tsp dried

225 to 500ml cups water

225g chopped boneless, skinless
chicken breasts

200g smoked sausage
cut into chunks

FOR CREOLE SAUCE

6 Tbsp unsalted butter

75g plain flour

500ml chicken/ or vegetable
stock

500ml Quick Tomato Sauce
(page 117)

1 tsp chilli powder

1/2 tsp cayenne pepper

1 tsp chili paste or Thai
curry paste

1 tsp coarsely ground black
pepper

1/2 tsp hot sauce

100g grated mozzarella cheese

100g grated Monterey Jack cheese

FOR CORNBREAD TOPPING:

75g coarse yellow cornmeal

170g plain flour

75g firmly packed light
brown sugar

1 tsp baking powder

1/4 tsp baking soda

1/2 tsp salt

1/2 tsp ground coriander

1 large egg, lightly beaten

350ml buttermilk

50ml vegetable oil

Preheat oven to 190°C/Gas Mark 5. Oil the sides and bottom of a 25 × 30-cm baking dish. In a large stockpot of boiling, salted water, cook the pasta sheets until *al dente*, about 10 minutes for dry, 2 to 3 minutes for fresh. Drain the pasta, rinse with cold water, and set aside on kitchen paper to dry.

In a large frying pan on medium-high heat, add 4 tablespoons of olive oil. When the oil is hot, add the celery, green peppers, red peppers and onion. Sauté until translucent and tender, about 5 minutes. Add the corn and continue to cook for an additional 2 minutes, then add the okra. Stir the okra into the mixture and continue to cook. The okra will begin to get gummy and possibly stick to the bottom of the pan. If the pan appears to be dry and the vegetables are sticking, add 225ml of water to moisten.

Continue to cook until the okra is tender and bright green, about 5 minutes. Add the thyme, sage and rosemary. At this point, if the mixture appears to be overly dry, again add up to 225ml of water and cook until a thick liquid forms. Remove the pan from the heat and set it aside. In a separate frying pan, heat the remaining 2 tablespoons of olive oil on medium to high heat. Add the

chicken and sausage, and cook until browned and cooked through, about 10 minutes. Add the chicken and sausage to the vegetable mixture and combine.

[To prepare the Creole sauce]
In a medium saucepan over medium to high heat, melt the butter and add the flour; using a whisk, stir continuously, cooking the mixture until a rich, dark brown colour is achieved, along with a nutty aroma. This is the roux (thickener) for the sauce. Add the chicken stock a little at a time, stirring vigorously after each addition to incorporate the liquid thoroughly and prevent lumps. Be careful of the initial steam that will rise from adding the stock. After all the chicken stock is incorporated, reduce the heat to low and add the tomato sauce; stir and cook for 5 minutes. Add the chilli powder, cayenne pepper, chilli paste, black pepper, and hot sauce, stir to incorporate, and continue to cook for 5 minutes. Remove the saucepan from the heat and set it aside.

[To prepare cornbread topping]
In a medium-sized mixing bowl, combine all the dry ingredients; using a whisk, stir them until thoroughly mixed. Pushing from the middle of the bowl outwards with a spoon, form a well in the centre of the dry ingredients.

Add the egg, buttermilk and oil in the well. Working from the sides inwards with the whisk, begin to incorporate the dry ingredients gradually, then whisk vigorously to combine the ingredients. The slow incorporation of the wet ingredients into the dry will prevent lumps from forming in the batter. Set aside for assembly.

[To assemble]
In your baking dish, place 350ml of Creole sauce, evenly coating the bottom of the pan; top with three sheets of pasta. Top pasta with half of the vegetable filling, and sprinkle with half of the mozzarella and Monterey Jack cheeses. Repeat the layers with pasta, then 100ml of sauce, pasta again, the remainder of the vegetable filling and finally the remainder of the cheese. Using your hands, firmly pack the lasagne layers in the dish, making room for the cornbread batter on top. Drizzle the cornbread batter over the top in a solid layer, evenly coating the top layer. You may not need all of the batter; this depends on the thickness of your layers. Place the baking dish on a large baking sheet to catch any drips. Bake on middle shelf of the oven, uncovered, for 20 minutes, or until the cornbread topping is golden

brown and firm to the touch. The sides will be bubbling. Remove from the oven and let rest for 10 minutes before serving. There should be remaining Creole sauce that can be heated and served over the top of each portion of lasagne.

8 fresh or dry lasagne sheets

3 Tbsp Thai fish sauce

3 Tbsp fresh lime juice

2 Tbsp sugar

1 Tbsp sesame oil

1 Tbsp olive oil

4 spring onions, sliced diagonally

75g grated carrot

2 cloves garlic, crushed

75g beansprouts

1 head Chinese leaves, cleaned and trimmed, cut in half lengthways and then chopped

1/4 tsp red pepper flakes

1 Tbsp fresh coriander, chopped, plus additional left whole for garnish

2 Tbsp chopped dry-roasted peanuts

900g soft tofu, drained

2 Tbsp fresh Italian parsley, finely chopped

2 Tbsp fresh basil, finely chopped

1/2 tsp turmeric

2 Tbsp Thai curry paste

50ml coconut milk, not shaken

2 Tbsp sugar

Preheat oven to 200°C/Gas Mark 6. Oil the bottom and sides of a 25 × 30-cm baking dish. In a large pot of boiling, salted water cook the lasagne sheets, 10 minutes for dry and 2 to 3 minutes for fresh. Remove from the water and rinse in cold water. Place them on kitchen paper to dry. In a small mixing bowl, combine the fish sauce, lime juice and sugar; set the mixture aside. Heat the sesame and olive oils in a large frying pan over medium to high heat. Add the onion, carrots and garlic, and stir-fry the vegetables until tender, about 2 minutes, being careful not to brown them.

Add the beansprouts and Chinese leaves, combine, and cook for an additional 2 to 4 minutes until wilted. Add the pepper flakes, coriander, and peanuts, and cook for 1 further minute. Add the fish sauce mixture, combine, and cook until the liquid is reduced by half, about 5 minutes.

Place the tofu in the bowl of a food processor fitted with the blade attachment. Process the tofu until a uniform creamy texture is obtained. Add the parsley, basil, turmeric, curry paste, coconut milk and sugar. Process until well combined. Remove the mixture from the processor and set it aside.

[To assemble]
Place two sheets of pasta on the bottom of your baking dish, cutting them to fit if necessary. Top with the vegetable mixture, then another layer of pasta, then the tofu mixture. Repeat the layers with pasta, vegetable mixture, pasta and finally the tofu mixture on top. Place in the oven and bake for 20 minutes, or until it begins to turn golden brown and crack. Remove from the oven and let rest for 10 minutes before cutting to serve.

[serves 6]

Thai Lasagne with Stir-Fried Vegetables and Curried Tofu

Here I have combined all the flavours of Pad Thai with crisp, fresh Asian vegetables with a creamy tofu filling to create a truly Eastern approach to lasagne.

While preparing sautéed baby spinach and rocket one evening, I chose to add some finely chopped artichoke hearts with feta and olives. This was a hit and subsequently became a filling for this tremendous lasagne. The flavours are intense and rich, with beautiful layers of varied ingredients.

[serves 8]

Lasagne **with Artichokes and Sautéed Greens**

2 medium bunches rocket, trimmed, washed and chopped

500g baby spinach, trimmed, washed and chopped

2 medium bunches Swiss chard, trimmed, washed and chopped

9 pasta sheets

500ml olive oil

4 garlic cloves, thinly sliced

8 anchovy fillets, chopped

50ml white wine

100g black olives, sliced

50g Kalamata olives, sliced

75g toasted pine kernels

700g bottled marinated artichoke hearts, drained and chopped

2 fresh tomatoes, seeded and chopped

2 Tbsp fresh marjoram leaves, chopped

1/4 tsp coarsely ground black pepper

1/4 tsp cayenne pepper

salt to taste

500g mascarpone cheese

225ml double cream

115g toasted bread crumbs

30g fresh Romano or Parmesan cheese, grated

Preheat oven to 220°C/Gas Mark 7. Evenly coat the bottom and sides of a 25 × 30-cm baking dish with cooking spray or olive oil. In a large pot of boiling, salted water, add the greens and blanch for 1 minute. Remove the greens from the water (reserving the water to cook the pasta in) and rinse it under cold water. Drain well, squeezing out any excess water. Chop into small pieces. In the same pot of boiling, salted water cook the pasta sheets for 10 minutes until *al dente*. Remove the pasta from the water and rinse it with cold water. Place on a towel to dry. In a large frying pan, heat the olive oil over medium heat. Add the garlic and anchovies, cooking them for 1 minute, being sure to break up the anchovies with a spoon as they cook. Increase the heat to medium to high, add the greens and sauté for 4 minutes. Add the wine and let it boil away. Add the black and Kalamata olives, toasted pine kernels, artichoke hearts,

tomatoes, marjoram leaves, black pepper, cayenne pepper, and salt if needed. Mix well and set aside. In a small saucepan, heat the mascarpone cheese with the cream over very low heat, until it just reaches a pourable consistency, about 1 minute. Remove the saucepan from the heat and season with salt and black pepper.

[To assemble]
Pour a thin layer of the mascarpone cream over the bottom of the baking dish. Add a layer of lasagne sheets, topping this with a layer of the greens mixture and a drizzle of mascarpone cream. Layer with more lasagne sheets, and top with the remaining greens and another drizzle of cream. End with pasta, the remaining cream and an even sprinkling of toasted bread crumbs. Cover with foil and bake for 20 minutes. Uncover and bake for an additional 15 minutes to brown the top. Remove from the oven and let stand for 10 minutes before cutting to serve.

Tips on Toasting Nuts

Toasting nuts is simple. Whether on the stove or in the oven, toasting is quick and produces an intensely concentrated flavour in the nuts that imparts a great, exotic taste to many dishes. Be careful to watch the nuts closely. This is the only tricky part, because they toast very quickly.

On the stove top, place the nuts in a medium frying pan over medium to high heat, tossing them in the pan continuously. The nuts will begin to brown and you will smell a nutty aroma. Remove them from the heat, place them on to a dish and let them cool.

To toast in the oven, preheat the oven to 200°C/Gas Mark 6, and place the nuts on an oven tray. Bake for about 5 minutes (time will vary depending on the nuts used). The nuts will begin to turn golden brown and exude a nutty aroma. Remove the tray from the oven and place the nuts on a separate dish to cool.

[Two important things to remember]

1. Oil is not needed to toast nuts, because their natural oils will assist in the process.
2. Removing the nuts immediately from the frying pan or oven tray is important so they don't continue to cook and burn. Remember, nuts have natural oils that have been heated up. When oil is hot, it cooks. The nuts can turn dark and burn before you know it.

2 Tbsp extra-virgin olive oil

8 lasagne sheets, cooked to
al dente

450g mushrooms (such as cremini
or Bella), stems removed,
cleaned and finely chopped
in a food processor

30g cup shallots, finely chopped

2 cloves garlic, crushed

salt and coarsely ground black
pepper

300g frozen chopped spinach,
defrosted and squeezed dry

1/4 tsp ground nutmeg

500g ricotta cheese

225ml chicken stock

225g Gorgonzola cheese,
crumbled

100ml double cream

2 Tbsp Italian parsley,
finely chopped

1 Tbsp fresh rosemary, chopped

170g grated mozzarella

50g freshly grated Parmesan
cheese

Preheat oven to 200°C/Gas Mark 6. Oil the bottom and sides of a 25 × 30-cm baking dish. In a large pot of boiling, salted water, cook the lasagne sheets until *al dente*, about 10 minutes. Remove the sheets from the water and rinse under cold water to cool. Set aside to dry.

Heat the olive oil in a medium frying pan over medium to high heat. Sauté the mushrooms, shallots and garlic until the mushrooms give off their juices and darken, and the shallots are tender, about 7 to 8 minutes.

Season with salt and black pepper. Add the spinach, heat through for 2 more minutes, add the nutmeg, and combine. Add the ricotta cheese, and stir into the mixture and heat the cheese through, about 1 additional minute. Remove the pan from the heat but leave the mixture in the warm pan.

In a small saucepan, heat the stock over medium to high heat. Add the Gorgonzola to the stock and melt it. Bring the liquid to a slow boil, and stir in the cream, cooking to thicken for about 2 minutes. Add the parsley and rosemary.

[To assemble]
Place cooked, dry lasagne sheets on a large, clean work surface. Spread an even layer of spinach filling down each lasagne sheet. Create the roulade by rolling the pasta, starting from one end and rolling tight to the other. Arrange the eight bundles, seam-side down, in a baking dish. Pour warm Gorgonzola sauce over roulades and top with mozzarella. Bake for 15 minutes or until the tops are golden brown. Heat the roulades under the grill if necessary to brown the tops. Remove from oven and let rest for 10 minutes before serving.

[serves 8]

Spinach and Mushroom Lasagne **Roulades with Gorgonzola Cream**

Rolling lasagne sheets with a delicious filling is an easy way to bring an elegant twist to a traditional dish. Generally any filling will work; just make sure that plenty of sauce is used on the top and bottom to prevent the pasta from drying out during baking.

FOR HEARTY MEAT SAUCE:

2 Tbsp olive oil

150g minced beef

150g minced turkey

150g minced pork sausage seasoned with sage

salt

freshly ground black pepper

2 medium onions, finely chopped

2 stalks celery, finely chopped

1 large carrot, finely chopped

2 Tbsp chopped garlic

1¹/₂ kg canned, peeled, seeded, and chopped tomatoes

75g canned, tomato purée

1¹/₃L beef stock or water

2 sprigs fresh thyme

2 bay leaves

3 tsp dried oregano or marjoram

3 tsp dried basil leaves

pinch of crushed red pepper

50g Parmigiano-Reggiano cheese

FOR CHEESE AND PASTA:

1 Tbsp olive oil

500g fresh ricotta cheese

175g grated provolone cheese

225g grated mozzarella cheese

30g cup grated Romano cheese

2 eggs

50ml milk

2 Tbsp fresh basil, chopped

1 Tbsp chopped garlic

salt

freshly ground black pepper

225g grated Parmigiano-Reggiano cheese

450g dried lasagne sheets, cooked according to package instructions

[serves 8]

Lasagne **with Hearty Meat Sauce**

A hearty dish for a cold winter night, this dish uses pork sausage and minced turkey as part of the meat sauce, with provolone cheese to round out the cheese filling.

[To prepare the meat sauce]

In a large, nonreactive saucepan, over medium heat, add the oil. When the oil is hot, add the meat and brown for 4 to 6 minutes. Season with salt and pepper, and mix well. Add the onions, celery, and carrots. Cook for 4 to 5 minutes or until the vegetables are soft. Add the garlic and tomatoes. Season with salt and pepper. Continue to cook for 2 to 3 minutes. In a medium-sized mixing bowl, whisk the tomato purée with the stock until combined. Add the canned tomatoes to the stock and purée mixture. Add the thyme, bay leaves, oregano, basil and red pepper. Mix well. Bring the liquid to the boil, reduce the heat to medium, and simmer for about 2 hours. Stir occasionally and add more liquid if needed. During the last 30 minutes of cooking, reseason with salt and pepper and stir in the cheese. Remove from the heat and let sit for 25 minutes before serving.

[To cook pasta and cheese]

Preheat the oven to 180°C/Gas Mark 4. Coat the sides and bottom of a 25 × 30-cm baking dish with 1 tablespoon of olive oil. In a large stockpot with ample salted, boiling water, cook the lasagne sheets according to the package directions. In a mixing bowl, combine the ricotta, provolone, mozzarella, grated Romano, egg, milk, basil and garlic. Mix well. Season with salt and pepper.

[To assemble]

Spread 150g of the meat sauce on to the bottom of the oiled baking dish. Sprinkle one quarter of the Parmigiano-Reggiano cheese over the sauce. Cover the cheese with one quarter of the cooked pasta. Spread one quarter of the cheese filling evenly over the pasta. Repeat the above process with the remaining ingredients, topping the lasagne with the remaining sauce. Place in the oven and bake until bubbly and golden, about 45 minutes to 1 hour. Remove from the oven and let rest for 10 minutes before serving. Slice and serve.

450g fresh lasagne sheets or 450g dried, cooked according to package directions

4 Tbsp olive oil

1 recipe Basic Pesto (page 118)

24 fresh sea scallops, cleaned

salt and pepper

500g teardrop or pear tomatoes, red or yellow, cut in half lengthways

450g fresh asparagus, trimmed and blanched

450g fresh shiitake or chanterelle mushrooms, cleaned

50g grated Parmigiano-Reggiano cheese

[serves 8]

Folded Lasagne with Grilled Sea Scallops

A simple "pile" of lasagne sheets makes the basis of the dish, with succulent grilled scallops lying atop and nestled in between the folded ribbons of pasta. While far removed from the traditional idea of lasagne layers, this dish exemplifies the importance of pesto in Italian cooking.

Bring a pan of salted water to the boil with 1 tablespoon of olive oil. If using fresh pasta, boil for approximately 2 minutes until *al dente*. If using dry, packaged pasta, cook according to package instructions. Remove from the water and drain. In a mixing bowl, toss the pasta with a tablespoon of the remaining olive oil. Season with salt and pepper. Set aside.

Preheat the grill. Season the scallops with a tablespoon of olive oil, salt and pepper. Place the scallops on the grill and cook for 2 to 3 minutes on each side or until the scallops are firm to the touch. In a sauté pan, over medium heat, add the remaining tablespoon of the oil.

When the oil is hot, add the tomatoes. Sauté for 2 minutes. Add the asparagus and mushrooms. Season with salt and pepper. Continue to sauté for 3 to 4 minutes or until the mushrooms are soft.

In a large mixing bowl, toss the pasta with the vegetables and pesto. Mix well. Add the cheese and mix well. Readjust the seasonings if necessary. Mound two sheets of pasta in a ribbonlike formation in the centre of each serving plate. Lay the scallops between and over the pasta sheets. Garnish with parsley and serve.

chapter 4

Vegetarian and
Lighter Lasagne

Bring a large pot of lightly salted water to the boil. Add the pasta and cook for 8 to 10 minutes or until *al dente*; drain and pat dry on a towel. In a large bowl, combine the ricotta cheese, eggs, Parmesan cheese, parsley, basil and ground black pepper. Stir to blend; set aside.

Heat oil in a large saucepan over high heat. Sauté the onions for about 5 minutes, stirring occasionally. Add the carrot slices and sauté for about 2 minutes. Then stir in the green pepper, red bell pepper and broccoli. Stir all the ingredients together, reduce the heat to medium and cook until tender, about 5 minutes. Scrape the veggies into the ricotta mix and combine thoroughly. Preheat the oven to 180°C/Gas Mark 4. Ladle 225ml of tomato sauce into a 25 x 30-cm baking dish and spread evenly over the bottom.

Place two sheets of lasagne lengthways in the dish, then spread about a litre of the filling over the pasta. Sprinkle half of the mozzarella cheese over the filling; repeat the layers. Bake in preheated oven for 1 hour. Let stand about 10 to 15 minutes to firm up before serving.

700g lasagne sheets

900g ricotta cheese

4 eggs

150g grated Parmesan cheese

3Tbsp chopped fresh parsley

2 tsp dried basil

Ground black pepper to taste

100ml olive oil

170g onion, chopped

150g carrots, sliced

50g green pepper, chopped

50g red pepper, chopped

450g chopped frozen broccoli, thawed and drained

700g Quick Tomato Sauce (page 117), Slow-Simmered Tomato Sauce (page 120), or your favourite chunky-style spaghetti sauce

200g mozzarella cheese, divided

[serves 9]

Classic Vegetarian Lasagne

This lasagne is so easy to prepare. In a culture where there are relatively few options for vegetarians, here is a great meatless recipe. With a generous amount of garden-fresh vegetables, this lasagne goes well with a salad and warm bread to make a hearty meal..

1 Tbsp extra-virgin olive oil

50g onion, finely chopped

30g celery, finely chopped

30g carrot, finely chopped

2 garlic cloves, crushed

1/2 tsp dried thyme

900g chopped plum tomatoes

3 Tbsp plus 2 Tbsp fresh basil, chopped

225g low-fat ricotta cheese

75g packed, grated low-fat mozzarella cheese, divided

pepper

8 fresh lasagne sheets, cooked and cut in half crossways

50g freshly grated Parmesan cheese

In a large frying pan, heat the oil over medium heat. Add the onions, celery, carrot, garlic and thyme, and sauté until the vegetables are tender and translucent, about 8 minutes. Add tomatoes with any juices; simmer until slightly thickened, about 8 minutes. Stir in 3 Tablespoons basil. Season with salt and pepper. In a small saucepan over medium-low heat, stir the ricotta cheese until just heated through. Add half of the packed mozzarella cheese. Stir just until melted, about 1 minute. Season to taste with pepper.

Preheat broiler to high. Spoon 50ml tomato sauce into the bottom of each of four shallow bowls. Place two hot lasagne sheet halves side by side atop the sauce in each bowl. Top with one quarter of the cheese mixture, then with two more pasta halves. Divide the remaining sauce among the bowls. Sprinkle with Parmesan and remaining mozzarella cheese and 2 tablespoons basil. Place under the grill for about 3 minutes until the mozzarella cheese begins to brown and bubble. Serve immediately in individual dishes.

[serves 4]

Classic Low-fat Lasagne

Even with the use of lighter ingredients, this combination has a great flavour. This lasagne is not only easy on the waistline—it also beats the clock. There is no baking, so it takes hardly any time to prepare.

In a large bowl, combine aubergine, courgettes, peppers, onions, garlic, rosemary, half of the basil, salt, pepper and 100ml olive oil and marinate for 2 to 3 hours at room temperature.

Preheat oven to 190°C/Gas Mark 5. Remove the vegetables from the marinade to a deep roasting tin. Roast in the oven until tender and browned, about 30 minutes, stirring twice during roasting time. In a frying pan, heat 2 tablespoons of olive oil. Add the mushrooms and sauté over medium heat for 3 minutes; add the baby spinach, sautéing until wilted and tender; set aside.

In a large pot of boiling, salted water, cook the lasagne sheets until *al dente*, 10 minutes for dry, 2 to 3 minutes for fresh. Drain and rinse with cold water. Dry on a towel.

[To assemble]
Pour a third of the Béchamel Sauce over the bottom of an oiled 25 x 30-cm baking dish, and arrange about one quarter of the roasted vegetable mixture on top. Cover with pasta, then top with one quarter more of vegetable mixture, add some mushrooms, some diced tomatoes, 100ml Béchamel Sauce, some of the remaining basil, and 100g Parmesan cheese. Repeat the procedure twice, ending with Parmesan cheese and 100ml Béchamel Sauce. Cover with foil and bake for 25 minutes. Remove the foil and bake for an additional 10 minutes until the lasagne is bubbling and golden brown. Remove from the oven and let rest for 10 minutes before cutting to serve.

1 aubergine, peeled and chopped

2 courgettes, chopped

1 red pepper, seeded and chopped

1 yellow pepper, seeded and chopped

1 small onion, chopped

2 garlic cloves, crushed

2 sprigs rosemary

75g fresh basil, shredded

salt and freshly ground black pepper

150ml extra-virgin olive oil

75g chopped fresh shiitake mushrooms

300g baby spinach

9 fresh or dry lasagne sheets

700ml Béchamel Sauce (page 113)

2 beef tomatoes, peeled, seeded and cubed

300g grated Parmesan cheese

[serves 6]

Vegetable Lasagne **with White Sauce**

Garden-fresh summer vegetables fill the layers of this vibrant vegetarian dish. The creamy Béchamel Sauce gives the lasagne the richness and moisture it needs while allowing the vegetables to take centre stage.

9 lasagne sheets, dried or fresh

1 Tbsp unsalted butter

2 Tbsp olive oil

2 shallots, chopped

3 cloves garlic, crushed

1 medium carrot, chopped

1 medium parsnip, chopped

300g mushrooms (such as Bella or crimini), thinly sliced

600g frozen broccoli, thawed, drained, and chopped, or 700g pounds fresh broccoli, trimmed, blanched, drained, and chopped

1 Tbsp fresh Italian parsley, finely chopped

salt and coarsely ground black pepper

700ml Béchamel Sauce (page 113)

100ml milk

450g Fontina cheese, grated

zest of one lemon

pinch of grated nutmeg

2 Tbsp fresh basil, chopped

150g grated Parmesan cheese

250g goat's cheese (such as Montrachet)

[serves 8]

Broccoli Lasagne **with Mushrooms and Fontina Cheese**

In this easy-to-prepare dish, robust Fontina cheese lends itself well to the crisp, garden-fresh taste of broccoli and the exotic flavours of the mushrooms.

Preheat oven to 200°C/Gas Mark 6. Evenly coat sides and bottom of a 25 × 30-cm baking dish with cooking spray or olive oil. In a large pot of boiling, salted water, cook the lasagne sheets until *al dente*, 10 minutes for dried, 2 to 3 minutes for fresh. Remove sheets from water, rinse under cold water and set aside on a towel to dry.

Melt the butter with the olive oil in a large sauté pan over medium to high heat. Sauté the shallots with the garlic, carrots and parsnips until the shallots begin to brown and the carrots and parsnips become tender, about 5 minutes. Add the mushrooms and continue to cook, allowing the mushrooms to sweat and wilt, about 4 minutes. Add the broccoli and parsley, stirring to combine. Continue to cook for an additional 2 minutes to heat broccoli through. Season with salt and pepper, remove from heat and set aside. In a medium-sized saucepan, heat the Béchamel Sauce. Add 100ml milk to thin, bring to a simmer, add Fontina cheese and lemon zest and cook over medium heat, stirring constantly until smooth and creamy and Fontina cheese is melted, about 15 minutes. Season with nutmeg and salt and pepper.

[To assemble]
In the baking dish, layer 225ml of the Fontina cheese sauce, three lasagne sheets, 225 ml more Fontina cheese sauce, half the broccoli-mushroom mixture, half the chopped basil, one third of the Parmesan cheese and one third of the goat's cheese. Top with three additional pasta sheets, half of the remaining Fontina cheese sauce, remaining broccoli-mushroom mixture, remaining basil, one third of the Parmesan cheese, and one third of the goat's cheese. Top with remaining three pasta sheets and Fontina cheese sauce, then sprinkle with the remaining Parmesan and goat's cheese. Cover with foil coated with cooking spray. Bake for 20 minutes, uncover, and bake for an additional 10 to 15 minutes until top is golden and bubbly. Remove from oven and let rest for 10 minutes before cutting to serve.

Roasted Asparagus Lasagne with Fontina Cheese

Fresh, oven-roasted asparagus is a favourite of mine with any dish. In this lasagne, I have combined the richness of Parmigiano cream sauce and Fontina cheese with the intense flavours of roasted asparagus and onions.

1kg medium asparagus, ends trimmed, stalks peeled and cut in half

1 large sweet onion, peeled, cut in half and thinly sliced

3 Tbsp extra-virgin olive oil

2 Tbsp unsalted butter

50ml fresh-squeezed lemon juice

2 tsp grated lemon peel

salt

coarsely ground black pepper

3 fresh savory sprigs, leaves chopped

2 fresh tarragon sprigs, leaves chopped

FOR THE PARMIGIANO SAUCE:

150g freshly grated Parmigiano-Reggiano cheese

500ml double cream

freshly grated nutmeg

3 Tbsp fresh chives, finely chopped

1 recipe Basic Pasta (page 122), cut for lasagne or 450g dry lasagne sheets

225g grated Fontina cheese

225g grated mozzarella cheese

Preheat the oven to 230°C/Gas Mark 8. Place the asparagus and onions on a large baking sheet. Drizzle with the olive oil, and dot with the butter. Sprinkle the lemon juice and zest on top and season with salt and coarsely ground black pepper. Mix the vegetables well with your hands, making sure they are evenly coated with the seasonings. Bake until soft and just starting to brown, about 20 minutes.

When the vegetables are tender and aromatic, remove them from the oven and sprinkle with the savory and tarragon. Toss to combine. The heat of the vegetables will wilt and concentrate the flavours of the herbs.

Lower the oven temperature to 220°C/Gas Mark 7. In a small saucepan, stir the Parmigiano-Reggiano cheese into the cream and mix well. Simmer gently over low heat until the cheese is melted and the sauce is fairly smooth (there will be a slight graininess to the sauce because of the texture of the cheese). Season with the nutmeg, black pepper and a pinch of salt. Add the chives and stir. If using fresh pasta, cook the lasagne sheets in a large pot of boiling, salted water until tender, about 2 minutes. If using dry sheets, cook them according to the package directions. Drain the sheets and rinse them with cold water, then lay them out in one layer on a towel to dry.

[To assemble]
Lightly coat a 20 × 20-cm baking dish with olive oil. Layer the bottom with pasta, and follow with a layer of asparagus and onion and a thin layer of grated Fontina and mozzarella cheese. Season lightly. Add another layer of pasta, and top with more asparagus, half of the Parmigiano cream sauce and another thin layer of Fontina and mozzarella cheeses. Repeat until you use up the ingredients, ending with a layer of pasta. Pour the remaining Parmigiano cream on top, letting it run down the sides a bit.

Cover the dish with foil and bake for about 20 minutes. Remove the foil and continue to bake until the top is golden and bubbling, about an additional 15 to 20 minutes. Remove from the oven and let rest for 10 minutes before cutting.

[Variations]
Roasting vegetables concentrates and intensifies their flavours. Vegetables such as aubergine, butternut squash, leeks, peppers, tomatoes and artichoke hearts are all great choices for roasting. Simply coat them in olive oil, toss with salt and black pepper and roast in a hot oven until tender and brown. Layer in lasagne with Quick Tomato Sauce (page 117) or with the Parmigiano cream sauce and cheeses in this recipe.

For an incredible variation replace either the Fontina or mozzarella cheese with their smoked counterpart. Smoking cheese intensifies the flavours, much as roasting vegetables does. In addition, it gives the cheese an earthy flavour of smoke.

A note on fresh herbs

Fresh herbs are like gold to any seasoned cook. The flavours and variations are endless. The contribution that fresh herbs make to any dish is immeasurable. Unfortunately, fresh herbs are not always available, depending on the time of year and your location or available supermarkets. When you can find fresh herbs, they can be easily frozen for later use. Simply wash and clean the herbs thoroughly, being sure to pick any dead or rotting leaves from the bunch. Dry the herbs completely, put on kitchen paper in a single layer, and roll the kitchen paper from end to end tightly. Place in an airtight container or freezer bag and freeze for later use. I do not suggest using frozen herbs in fresh sauces such as pesto, however; make the pesto when fresh herbs are available and freeze it.

In the case of basil and hard-stemmed, broad-leaved herbs, remove the leaves from the stems, freezing only the leaves of the plant.

Substituting herbs
[Dried for fresh]

In some cases, dried herbs are needed when fresh are not available. When using dried herbs, remember one simple rule: Use half as much of the dried as you would of the fresh. The flavours of dried herbs are concentrated and harsher than those of fresh, so less is needed.

[One herb for another]

Sometimes, when a recipe calls for one herb that is not available fresh, but dried is not desirable, there may be a fresh herb that can be substituted. For example, in the recipe for Roasted Asparagus Lasagne with Fontina Cheese, savory and tarragon are called for. In this case, if one or the other is not available, just increase the quantity of the one that is available to equal the quantity of the two. A herb like savory is similar in smell and flavour to oregano and marjoram. So, one of those could also be substituted if the other is not available. Generally, a recipe will tell you if dried can be used or if there is an alternative to the fresh one. And remember, you can always ask your local greengrocer for advice.

500g courgettes

500g summer squash

5 large carrots, peeled

50ml plus 2 Tbsp extra-virgin olive oil

1 Tbsp black pepper

1 medium aubergine

2 portobello mushrooms, stems removed, wiped clean with a damp cloth

FOR THE CHEESE FILLING:

450g ricotta cheese

225g feta cheese, crumbled

4 Tbsp packed fresh basil leaves, thinly sliced

1 egg

450g dry lasagne sheets

1 recipe Fire-Roasted Red Pepper Sauce (page 114)

175g baby spinach

225g grated mozzarella cheese

[serves 9]

Grilled Vegetable Lasagne **with Fire-Roasted Red Pepper Sauce**

I love to grill vegetables no matter the occasion or time of year. While it is a bit more time consuming, the taste is tremendous. There is no substitute for the intensity that fire imparts to the flavours of vegetables.

[To prepare the vegetables]
Wash and clean all the vegetables, and slice the squash, courgettes and carrots diagonally about 5mm thick. In a large bowl, toss the sliced squash, courgettes and carrots with 2 tablespoons olive oil and 1 tablespoon black pepper, coating it evenly. Set aside. Peel the aubergine and slice it into 5mm thick rounds. Place the aubergine and the whole mushrooms on a plate and coat them evenly with the remaining 50ml of olive oil. On a hot outdoor grill or stove-top grill pan, grill the vegetables.

Grill the squash, courgettes, carrots and aubergine for about 7 minutes on each side; grill the mushrooms for about 20 minutes on each side. Grilling times will vary depending on the cooking surface and the appliance.

When grilling is complete, set all the vegetables aside for assembly, except the mushrooms. The mushrooms need to be sliced thinly.

[To prepare the cheese filling]
In a large mixing bowl, combine the ricotta cheese, feta cheese, basil and egg. Set aside.

[To assemble]
Preheat the oven to 180°C/Gas Mark 4. Oil the bottom and sides of a 25 × 30-cm baking dish.

If using dry pasta sheets, prepare them according to package directions. If using fresh pasta, boil it in an ample amount of boiling, salted water for 2 to 3 minutes. Remove the

sheets from the water and run them under cold water until cooled. Set aside on kitchen paper to dry. Using about 100ml red pepper sauce, evenly coat the bottom of the baking dish. Top the sauce with an even layer of lasagne sheets, being careful not to overlap them. Cut the sheets to fit the pan if necessary. Top the pasta with half of the baby spinach in an even layer, then with half of the vegetables, alternating the vegetables in an even layer. Top the vegetables with a sprinkling of half of the mozzarella cheese, then with another layer of pasta sheets. Evenly coat them with half of the ricotta cheese mixture. Top with another layer of pasta, then the remaining spinach, grilled vegetables, and mozzarella cheese. Add three additional lasagne sheets. Top the lasagne with the remaining red pepper sauce. Cover the pan and bake for 30 minutes. Uncover and bake an additional 15 to 20 minutes until the sauce is browned.

900g broccoli rabe or broccoli

225g ricotta cheese

225g feta cheese

¼ tsp dried oregano leaves

½ tsp fresh rosemary leaves

⅛ tsp freshly grated nutmeg

3 egg whites

1 egg yolk

50ml milk, full cream or
semi-skimmed

30g bread crumbs

salt and pepper

450g lasagne sheets

100ml extra-virgin olive oil

1L Béchamel Sauce (page 113)

100g freshly grated
Parmesan cheese

100g butter or margarine

[To prepare the rabe]

Wash and clean the rabe carefully and chop coarsely. In a large pan, sauté the rabe in 3 tablespoons of olive oil for about 5 minutes until it is tender and bright green in colour. Remove the rabe from the heat and place it in a colander over the sink to drain. Chop the rabe either by hand or in a food processor so that it is chopped very finely but not puréed.

[To prepare the remainder of the filling]

Place the chopped rabe in a large mixing bowl. Add the ricotta cheese, feta cheese, oregano, rosemary, grated nutmeg, egg whites and yolk, and milk. Mix thoroughly. Add the bread crumbs and combine. Set aside for 10 to 15 minutes, while the bread crumbs absorb the liquids. Check the consistency after this time, adding water or bread crumbs, depending upon whether the mixture seems too loose or too dry. Season it with salt and pepper.

While the mixture is resting, cook the lasagne sheets in a large amount of water with salt and oil, according to the package directions. Once they are *al dente*, drain them and mix them with the olive oil to keep them from sticking together.

[To assemble]

Preheat the oven to 180°C/Gas Mark 4. Grease the bottom and sides of a 25 × 30-cm baking dish. Place one layer of pasta sheets on the bottom of the dish and cover with about 1 cm of the filling mixture. Ladle about 100ml of Béchamel Sauce over the pasta, and sprinkle freshly grated Parmesan cheese over this layer. Cover with another layer of pasta. Repeat the process by alternating layers of pasta, filling and Béchamel Sauce until the dish is full, with the last layer being pasta. Sprinkle olive oil and Parmesan cheese on the top. Dot with butter and bake for 45 minutes. Remove from the oven. Let rest for 10 to 15 minutes before slicing to serve. Cover each serving with warmed Béchamel Sauce.

[serves 6 to 8]

Broccoli Rabe Lasagne

Broccoli rabe has a bitter taste that's not for every palate. In this dish, I have added fresh herbs and nutmeg to balance the flavour of the rabe and have used feta cheese to impart a creamy, exotic taste.

When developing this recipe, I wanted to combine the garden-fresh flavours of salad greens with the crisp textures of spring vegetables. Instead of a typical ricotta cheese layer, I created a risotto-style filling with fresh herbs and goat's cheese.

Spring Vegetable Lasagne with Herbed Cream

FOR VEGETABLE FILLING:

2 Tbsp unsalted butter

2 Tbsp olive oil

200g fresh courgette, finely chopped

100g asparagus, trimmed, cut into 2.5-cm lengths

200g fresh fennel bulbs, finely chopped

1 medium onion, finely chopped

100g carrot, finely chopped

4 cloves garlic, crushed

150g shiitake mushrooms, thinly sliced

75g raddichio, finely shredded

salt and coarsely ground black pepper

450g fresh baby spinach

FOR RISOTTO FILLING:

1 Tbsp unsalted butter

1 Tbsp olive oil

200g Arborio rice

225ml dry white wine

1L chicken or vegetable stock

2 Tbsp finely chopped Italian parsley

75g freshly grated Parmigiano-Reggiano cheese

100g goat's cheese

salt and coarsely ground black pepper

FOR HERBED CREAM:

4 Tbsp unsalted butter

4 Tbsp plain flour

100ml dry white wine

500ml chicken or vegetable stock

3 Tbsp fresh basil, finely chopped

2 Tbsp fresh tarragon, finely chopped

3 Tbsp fresh chives, finely chopped

1 Tbsp fennel tops, finely chopped

1 tsp grated orange zest

225ml double cream

salt and coarsely ground black pepper

12 sheets fresh or dried lasagne

300g fresh mozzarella cheese, thinly sliced

Preheat oven to 200°C/Gas Mark 4. Evenly coat a 25 × 30-cm baking dish with cooking spray or olive oil. In a large pot of salted, boiling water, cook the pasta sheets, 10 minutes for dried or 2 to 3 minutes for fresh. Remove from water, rinse under cold water, drain, and set aside on paper towels to dry. For vegetable filling, melt 1 tablespoon butter with 1 tablespoon olive oil in a large frying pan over medium to high heat. Sauté courgette, asparagus, fennel, onion, carrot and garlic until tender and just beginning to colour, about 15 minutes. Add shiitake mushrooms and radicchio. Combine and cook until wilted, about 3 minutes. Season with salt and pepper. Remove from heat and transfer to a platter. In the same pan, heat the remaining tablespoon of butter and oil. Add the baby spinach, stirring to heat and wilt, about 2 minutes. Remove from heat and transfer to a platter.

[For risotto]
Melt butter with olive oil in a medium frying pan over medium to high heat. Add the rice, coating it with butter and oil, stirring constantly to lightly brown, about 5 minutes. Add the wine and incorporate; cook until all the wine has evaporated, about 5 minutes. Begin adding chicken stock to pan 100ml at a time. Between additions of stock, cook until it has evaporated, stirring periodically to combine. The rice will begin to plump up and become tender. Continue this process of adding stock and cooking until all the stock has been used up. At this time, the rice should have almost tripled in volume and be very fluffy and tender with a creamy consistency. If not, continue to add water or stock until a creamy consistency is reached. Remove from heat and transfer to a bowl. Add the parsley, Parmigiano-Reggiano, and goat's cheese. Stir to combine and melt cheeses. Add the salt and pepper to taste. Set aside to cool.

[For herbed cream]
Melt butter in a medium-sized saucepan over medium to high heat. Add flour and whisk to combine. Whisk continuously, cooking flour to a golden brown colour. Combine the wine and stock together in a bowl. Gradually add the wine and stock mixture to the flour mixture, whisking constantly to combine. Add the liquid slowly to prevent lumps. Be careful of the steam that will rise from the pan at the initial addition of the liquid. After the addition of all the wine-stock mixture, add the basil, tarragon, chives, fennel tops and orange zest. Stir to combine. Lower the heat to medium and continue to cook for about 2 minutes. Add the cream and simmer for 5 additional minutes. Season with salt and pepper. Remove from the heat.

[To assemble lasagne]
Begin with about 225ml of herbed cream on the bottom of the baking dish. Top with three sheets of pasta, and layer with half of the spinach, then half of the vegetable mixture. Top the vegetables with 225ml of herbed cream, and add one third of the mozzarella cheese. Repeat with three pasta sheets. Add all of the risotto mixture in an even layer. If the risotto appears to be too dry after cooling, add about 50ml of double cream or milk to moisten it. Top the risotto with another layer of three pasta sheets. Layer with remaining spinach, remaining vegetable mixture, about 225ml of herbed cream, and one third of the fresh mozzarella. Top with the last three pasta sheets, then add the remaining herbed cream, finishing with the remaining mozzarella cheese. Bake uncovered for 30 minutes or until the top is bubbling and golden brown. Remove from the oven and let rest for 10 minutes before cutting to serve.

2 Tbsp olive oil

1 medium onion, thinly sliced

2 Tbsp garlic, crushed

10 Roma tomatoes, seeded, cut into chunks

2 tsp fresh rosemary, finely chopped

1 tsp fresh oregano, finely chopped

2 Tbsp fresh basil, finely chopped

6 dried lasagne sheets, cooked according to pacage instructions

4 russet potatoes, sliced 3mm thick

salt and pepper

115g grated Swiss cheese

115g grated Gruyere cheese

1 Tbsp butter

50g toasted bread crumbs

Preheat oven to 230°C/Gas Mark 8. Spray a deep 25 × 30-cm dish with cooking spray. Sauté the onions in a frying pan over medium-high heat with olive oil until just soft. Stir in the garlic, and cook another minute until aromatic. Add the tomatoes, rosemary, oregano and basil. Continue to cook until all moisture has evaporated, about 10 minutes.

[Toasting bread crumbs]
In a frying pan (preferably Teflon-coated), melt 1 tablespoon butter. Add the bread crumbs and combine, stirring to coat evenly while cooking. Cook until golden brown and aromatic, about 5 minutes. Remove from the heat and allow to cool.

[To assemble]
Layer one third of the lasagne sheets in the prepared dish. Top with half of the sliced potatoes, and season with salt and pepper. Top the potatoes with half of the tomato mixture and sprinkle with half the cheeses. Repeat the layering, ending with cheese. Sprinkle evenly with toasted bread crumbs. Cover the gratin with foil and bake for 30 minutes. Remove the foil and bake for an additional 15 to 20 minutes to brown the cheese. Let stand 5 minutes to set the cheese before slicing and serving.

[serves 6 as a meal or 8 as a side dish]

Potato Gratin Lasagne

This is an adaptation of a great vegetable side dish. The lasagne sheets give it more layers and a firm consistency. Cut it into smaller portions and serve it as a side dish with roasted chicken. Larger portions served with a salad make a great vegetarian meal.

Preheat oven to 200°C/Gas Mark 6. Combine the mushrooms, onion, garlic, basil and parsley in a large baking dish. Drizzle with olive oil. Toss everything with your hands to coat evenly and combine. Top with chunks of butter. Pour the chicken stock over the vegetables, then add the cayenne pepper and coriander. Place in the oven and cook, uncovered, until the vegetables are tender and beginning to brown, about 20 to 30 minutes. Remove from the heat and set aside. In a large mixing bowl, combine the Asiago and mozzarella cheeses and set it aside.

[To assemble]

In a well-oiled 25 × 30-cm baking dish, place 225ml of the Quick Tomato Sauce on the bottom. Top with three lasagne sheets, and place half of the mushroom mixture on top of the sheets, topping with half of the rocket and then with about one third of the grated cheeses. Top the cheeses with pasta sheets, add 350ml sauce and repeat the layers with the remaining mushroom mixture, one third of the cheeses and the remaining rocket. Add the remaining three lasagne sheets, and top with the remaining tomato sauce and cheeses. Place in the oven and bake until bubbly and golden, about 45 minutes.

Ingredients
1¹/₃ kg portobello mushrooms, sliced
1 large onion, cut in half and thinly sliced
3 cloves garlic, crushed
fresh basil, thinly sliced
2 Tbsp Italian parsley, finely chopped
4 Tbsp extra-virgin olive oil
2 Tbsp unsalted butter
225ml chicken stock
¹/₂ tsp cayenne pepper
¹/₂ tsp ground coriander
225g Asiago cheese or aged parmesan cheese, grated
225g mozzarella cheese, grated
500ml Quick Tomato Sauce (page 117)
450g lasagne sheets cooked according to package instructions
284g rocket

[serves 9]

Roasted Portobello and Caramelised Onion Lasagne

This is a light dish with the robust, earthy flavours of roasted portobello mushrooms. The only cheeses in this dish are the grated Asiago and mozzarella. There is no heavy layer of ricotta or creamy sauce, just fresh mushrooms and rocket.

2 tsp olive oil

250g chopped leeks (about 4)

1 Tbsp chopped fresh or
1 tsp dried rubbed sage

4 garlic cloves, crushed

850g peeled butternut squash
in 1-cm cubes

100ml dry white wine

100ml water

1/4 tsp black pepper

300gl frozen chopped spinach,
thawed, drained and squeezed dry

FOR THE SAUCE:

2 Tbsp unsalted butter
or margarine

3 Tbsp plain flour

550ml cups milk

50g block-style cream cheese

1/4 tsp ground nutmeg

1/8 tsp black pepper

150g cups mozzarella cheese

50g grated sharp
provolone cheese

12 cooked lasagne sheets

sage sprigs for garnish

[To prepare vegetable filling]
Heat the oil in a large, nonstick frying pan over medium heat. Add the leeks, sage and garlic. Sauté 5 minutes. Add the squash, wine and water. Cover and cook for 20 minutes or until the squash is tender, stirring occasionally. Stir in 1/4 teaspoon pepper and the spinach.

[To prepare sauce]
In a large saucepan over medium-high heat, melt the butter, add the flour and whisk the mixture until combined. Cook for 3 minutes to brown the flour. Gradually add the milk to the flour mixture, whisking continuously to prevent lumps. Reduce the heat to medium, and cook until thick (about 10 minutes), stirring constantly. Remove the saucepan from the heat; add the cream cheese, nutmeg and half of the pepper, stirring with the whisk. Combine the mozzarella and provolone, and set aside.

[To assemble]
Preheat the oven to 200°C/gas Mark 6. Oil the sides and bottom of a 25 x 30-cm baking dish. Spread 100ml of sauce on the bottom, arrange the pasta sheets over the sauce, and top with 500ml of vegetable filling, 50g of the cheese mixture, and 100ml of sauce. Repeat the layers, ending with the pasta. Spread the remaining sauce over the pasta. Cover and bake for 30 minutes. Uncover, sprinkle with 50g of the cheese mixture, and bake an additional 10 minutes. Let stand for 10 minutes prior to cutting to serve. Garnish with sage sprigs, if desired.

[serves 8]

Butternut Squash and Spinach Lasagne

The best time to make this lasagne is when butternut squash is ripe—straight form the autumn harvest. The creamy texture of the squash combines well with spinach and leeks in this dish.

chapter 5

Breakfast Lasagne

Preheat oven to 200°C/Gas Mark 6. Coat a 20 × 20-cm baking dish with nonstick cooking spray. In a large pot of boiling, salted water, cook the lasagne sheets until *al dente*, 10 minutes for dried, 2 to 3 minutes for fresh. Remove from the water and rinse with cold water. Place on a towel to dry thoroughly.

In a large frying pan over medium to high heat, melt 2 tablespoons butter, and add the onion, red and green pepper and broccoli. Sauté until tender and onions are translucent, being careful not the brown them, about 10 minutes. Add the smoked ham and continue to cook for an additional 3 minutes. Season with salt and pepper. Remove from the heat and set aside.

In a small frying pan over medium to high heat, melt 1 tablespoon butter. Add the potatoes, cooking until golden brown, about 10 minutes.

Season with salt and pepper, and toss with the parsley. Remove from the heat.

In a medium bowl, beat together the eggs and the double cream, salt and pepper.

[To assemble]
Place two sheets of pasta on the bottom of the baking dish, top with half of the vegetable mixture, then sprinkle with one third of the Cheddar cheese. Top again with lasagne sheets, then with browned potatoes. Repeat with the sheets, the vegetable mixture, one third of the cheese, the last layer of pasta, then the bread cubes. Pour the beaten eggs over the bread cubes, and top with the remaining Cheddar cheese. Bake for 40 minutes or until the egg topping is golden and firm. Remove from the oven, and let rest for 10 minutes before cutting to serve. Serve with warmed Béchamel Sauce.

8 lasagne sheets, dry or fresh

2 Tbsp butter

50g onion, chopped

50g red pepper, chopped

50g green pepper, chopped

75g broccoli florets, chopped small

450g smoked ham, sliced thickly and chopped

salt and pepper

1 Tbsp butter

1 potato, peeled and grated

1 tsp fresh Italian parsley, finely chopped

3 eggs

2 Tbsp double cream

1/4 tsp salt

1/4 tsp coarsely ground black pepper

2 thick slices day-old French bread, cut into 2.5-cm cubes, tossed with 3 Tbsp melted butter

350g grated Cheddar cheese

350ml Béchamel Sauce (page 113)

[serves 6]

Baked Egg Strata Lasagne

This is a layered take on the classic one-dish breakfast. The flavours of the vegetables layered with potatoes and Cheddar are intense. Enjoy with toast and fruit.

FOR SIMPLE BUTTERMILK SCONES:

225g self-raising flour

50g shortening

225ml buttermilk, well chilled

1/4 cup butter

FOR HAM AND GRAVY:

1 Tbsp bacon fat or unsalted butter

6 slices moist, uncooked country ham or other smoked ham, about 8mm thick

1½ tsp unbleached plain flour

225ml fresh hot coffee

1/4 cup warm water

2 tsp brown sugar

Cayenne pepper to taste

Few drops of hot sauce to taste

Salt and freshly ground pepper

6 eggs, scrambled or fried

6 thin slices Cheddar cheese

Preheat oven to 240°C/Gas Mark 9. Combine the flour and shortening in a medium-sized mixing bowl with a pastry blender until the mixture is crumbly. Add the buttermilk, stirring just until the dry ingredients are moistened. Turn the dough out onto a lightly floured surface. Lightly dust the dough with flour, then roll or pat the dough to a 1-cm thickness. Cut dough with a 6-cm pastry cutter, trying to get as many biscuits as possible, since they toughen if the dough is rerolled. Your dough should yield twelve biscuits. Do not twist the cutter (as seems to be natural for many people), as it twists the dough, resulting in an uneven scone. Place in a greased 25 x 30-cm baking dish. Top each unbaked scone with a small pat of cold butter. Bake on the centre shelf of the oven for 12 to 14 minutes until raised and golden brown.

Meanwhile, in a large, heavy frying pan over medium to high heat, melt the fat. (A well-seasoned, cast-iron pan is preferred due solely to the flavours it imparts to the gravy). Slash the edges of the ham's exterior fat to keep the slices from curling while cooking. Fry the ham slices in batches until lightly browned in spots and a bit crispy around the edges, about 2 minutes per side. Arrange the ham slices on a platter when they are done. Keep the ham warm and reserve the pan juices in the frying pan.

[serves 6]

Simple Buttermilk Scone Stack with Country Ham and Red-Eye Gravy

This traditional breakfast from the southern states of America is a must-have on blustery winter mornings by the fire. Red-eye gravy is a staple Georgian breakfast condiment, using a cup of coffee to liven it up!

While the scones are baking, finish the gravy. Reheat the pan juices over medium heat and whisk in the flour. Pour in the coffee and scrape up any browned bits from the bottom of the pan. Add at least 50ml of warm water; use more for a milder coffee. Season the gravy with brown sugar and cayenne pepper. Taste the gravy and add salt, pepper, and hot sauce as needed.

[To assemble stacks]
Slice the biscuits in half. Place the biscuit bottoms back in the baking dish. Layer with sliced ham, cooked egg and cheese. Place the tops of the biscuits back on. Place in the oven and bake for 10 minutes until the cheese begins to melt and run down the sides. Serve with a side dish of red-eye gravy.

Liasagna

In a medium-sized saucepan, melt 6 tablespoons of butter over medium heat. Add the walnuts to the butter and "toast" them for about 2 minutes until you smell a nutty aroma. Add the bananas, brown sugar, 50ml maple syrup, 1/2 teaspoon cinnamon and 1/4 teaspoon nutmeg. Reduce the heat to low and let the sauce cook until the bananas become tender and the sauce is thick.

In a large mixing bowl, beat together the milk, cream, eggs, remaining cinnamon and vanilla.

Heat a lightly oiled griddle or frying pan over medium-high heat. Dunk each slice of bread in the mixture, soaking both sides. Place on the griddle and cook both sides until golden brown. When serving, lay one slice of French toast on a warmed plate, top with a scoop of the banana compote, layer with another slice of bread, and repeat with banana compote. Finish with one last piece of French toast. Arrange banana slices in a flower-petal configuration, overlapping them in a circular pattern. Top with fresh whipped cream and fresh orange zest.

[Variation]
When in season, fresh blue-berries are delicious. Reduce the bananas by one and add 50g fresh blueberries for a refreshing seasonal treat.

6 Tbsp unsalted butter
50g chopped walnuts
4 ripe bananas, peeled and sliced
2 Tbsp packed brown sugar
75ml maple syrup plus additional for serving
1/2 tsp ground cinnamon plus another 1/2 tsp
1/4 tsp ground nutmeg, divided
150ml milk
100ml whipping cream or half-and-half
3 eggs
1 tsp vanilla extract
12 thin slices white bread
fresh whipped cream
orange zest

[serves 4]

French Toast Lasagne with Banana-Walnut Compote

For breakfast, the French toast replaces pasta sheets to create this delightful comfort food. Use thinly sliced bread to achieve multiple layers while avoiding too much of a good thing.

MAKE THREE BATCHES OF
THE FOLLOWING:

3 eggs, lightly beaten

50gflour

1/4 tsp salt

225ml milk

1 Tbsp fresh chives,chopped

1 Tbsp fresh basil, chopped

3 Tbsp butter

FOR THE FILLING:

5 Tbsp olive oil

1 Tbsp unsalted butter

3 medium ripe tomatoes, seeded
and chopped

1 medium yellow, orange or red
pepper, chopped

300g mushrooms, sliced thinly

4 spring onions, thinly sliced

3 cloves fresh garlic, crushed

300g fresh baby spinach

2 Tbsp fresh Italian
parsley, chopped

350g minced breakfast sausage

100g grated Cheddar cheese

100g grated mozzarella
cheese, or 225g grated
Cheddar cheese

Preheat oven to 230°C/Gas Mark 8. In a medium-sized mixing bowl, whisk the eggs with the flour until creamy and free of lumps. Add the salt and milk, 100ml at a time, whisking to combine. Add the chives and basil, and incorporate them. You will need three separate batches of the egg mixture to complete the dish. Do not make three batches at once, as it is difficult to incorporate the flour all at once.

Place three 23-cm round cake tins in the oven for 5 minutes. Remove the tins from the oven, and coat them evenly with cooking spray. Add 1 tablespoon of butter to each pan, and return the tins to the oven to melt butter, about 1 to 2 minutes. Remove the tins from the oven and rotate to coat with butter. Pour the batter evenly into tins.

Return the tins to the oven and bake uncovered for 7 minutes. Reduce the heat to 170°C/Gas Mark 4 and bake for an additional 5 minutes until brown. The batter will become very fluffy as it bakes. When removed from the oven and allowed to rest, the omelette will fall to a thinner size. If possible, bake all three at once, so that assembly is quick.

While the batter is baking, melt the butter with the oil in a large sauté pan over medium to high heat. Sauté the tomato, pepper, mushrooms, spring onions, and garlic until tender. Do not brown or overcook. The vegetables should be tender with vibrant colour. Remove them from the pan and set them aside for assembly. Heat an additional 2 tablespoons of olive oil. Add the baby spinach and heat through until wilted and vibrant green. Do not overcook. Remove it from the pan and set it aside for assembly. In the same sauté pan, brown the sausage, breaking it up as it cooks. Remove it from the heat and set it aside for assembly. In a medium-sized mixing bowl, combine the Cheddar and mozzarella cheese, and parsley.

[To assemble]
Place one omelette in either a cake tin previously used for the omelette or in an ovenproof serving platter. Top the omelette with half of the spinach, then one third of the cheese mixture. Top the cheese evenly with half of the vegetable mixture, then half of the ground sausage. Place a second omelette on top. Repeat the layers with the remaining spinach, one third of the cheese, the remaining vegetables, and the sausage. Top with the third omelette, herb-side up. Finish with the remaining cheese. Place the layered dish in the oven to melt the cheeses, about 10 minutes. Use the grill to melt the top layer of cheese, if necessary. Remove from the oven, slice into pie-shaped pieces, and serve. Accompany it with breakfast potatoes and juice.

[serves 6 to 8]

Baked Omelette Lasagne

This is probably the most hearty breakfast dish I have seen in a while. Thick layers of fluffy herbed omelettes with sautéed vegetables and melted cheese make this a towering breakfast meal.

chapter 6

Dessert Lasagne

6 dried lasagne sheets

8 Gala or Golden Delicious apples, cored, peeled, and sliced

75g plain flour, divided

225g sugar, divided

100g packed brown sugar, divided

1½ tsp cinnamon, divided

¾ tsp nutmeg, divided

500g ricotta cheese

225g cheddar cheese, grated

1 egg

1 tsp vanilla extract

50g old-fashioned oats

3 Tbsp unsalted butter or margarine

Cook the pasta sheets according to the package directions, then drain. Preheat the oven to 180°C/Gas Mark 4. In a large bowl, mix the apples, 30g flour, 170g brown sugar, 1 teaspoon cinnamon, and ½ teaspoon nutmeg. In another bowl mix the cheeses and the egg. Spread half of the apple filling over bottom of a 25 × 30-cm baking dish. Layer with three pasta sheets, then the cheese mixture. Layer again with the remaining sheets and apple filling.

Wipe out the medium-sized bowl and use it to mix the oats, remaining 30g flour, 50g brown sugar, 1 cup sugar, ½ teaspoon cinnamon and ¼ teaspoon nutmeg. Using a pastry cutter or your fingers, cut in the butter until the mixture is crumbly. Sprinkle it evenly over the top of the lasagne sheet. Bake the lasagne until golden brown and the apples are tender, 45 to 50 minutes. Remove from oven and let rest 10 minutes before slicing to serve.

[serves 8 to 10]

Fresh Apple Dessert Lasagne

Crisp, juicy apples fresh from the autumn trees are my favourite. This recipe takes on the traditional apple crisp as a unique way to incorporate lasagne sheets. The firmness and thick texture of the pasta lends a stability to the dish that makes presentation a cinch. Serve it with a scoop of your favourite vanilla ice cream, and you have a year-round winner.

50g melted butter

14 sheets filo pastry dough

Sugar

FOR LEMON CREAM:

170ml fresh lemon juice

1 tsp unflavoured gelatine

6 Tbsp unsalted butter

2 Tbsp plus 2 tsp
lemon peel, grated

3 large eggs

3 large egg yolks

170g sugar

225ml chilled whipping cream

FOR CANDIED CITRUS STRIPS
AND SLICES:

1 large grapefruit

2 oranges

2 lemons

350ml water

150g sugar

$1/8$ tsp vanilla

$1^1/2$ Tbsp light golden syrup

FOR SIMPLE WHIPPED CREAM:

600ml whipping cream

$1/2$ tsp vanilla

2 Tbsp sugar

Preheat oven to 200°C/Gas Mark 6. Coat a large baking sheet evenly with butter. Unroll the filo dough. Place one sheet on a clean, dry work surface and spread it with melted butter. Place another sheet on top and spread it with butter. Repeat until you have a total of seven sheets layered with butter. Cut the sheets into eight equal squares, approximately 10 × 10-cm. Repeat the process with another set of filo sheets so that you have a total of sixteen 10 × 10-cm squares. (Filo dough will dry out very quickly if not kept covered. Moisten a tea towel with water and use it to cover the filo dough between usage.) Dust the top layer of each piece with granulated sugar, place in oven, and bake for 20 minutes or until golden brown.

Place 1 tablespoon of lemon juice in small bowl, and sprinkle gelatine over it. Let it stand about 10 minutes. Stir the butter, lemon peel and remaining lemon juice in a small saucepan over low heat until the butter melts. Whisk the eggs, yolks and sugar in a medium-sized metal bowl to blend. Gradually whisk in the butter mixture. Set the bowl over a saucepan of simmering water (do not let the bottom of the bowl touch the water). Whisk constantly until the mixture is thick and the thermometer registers 60°C for 3 minutes (about 8 minutes total). Remove from the water. Add the gelatine mixture to the hot lemon curd and whisk until the gelatine dissolves. Chill to room temperature, stirring often, about 30 minutes. Beat the cream in a large bowl until medium peaks form. Fold the whipped cream into the curd. Cover and chill at least 4 hours and up to 2 days.

[To prepare citrus strips]
With a vegetable peeler, remove the zest from the grapefruit, orange and lemon in long pieces. With a sharp knife, remove any white pith from the pieces. Add the strips of citrus zest to a 3-litre saucepan half filled with cold water; and bring it to the boil. Simmer for 10 minutes, and drain in sieve. In a heavy saucepan bring the water, sugar, vanilla and golden syrup to the boil, stirring until the sugar is dissolved. Add the strips and simmer gently over low heat until translucent and the syrup is thickened, 15 to 20 minutes. Cool the strips in the syrup. Keep the candied strips covered and chilled for up to 2 weeks.

[To make simple whipped cream]
Mix ingredients in a medium-sized metal bowl and beat until soft peaks form. Sugar and vanilla may be adjusted to taste.

[To assemble]
Put one square of the filo on a serving plate. Spread it with whipped cream, the lemon cream and finally the candied citrus strips. Top with filo, repeating twice, ending with a final layer of filo dough. Garnish the top of each lasagne with a dollop of whipped cream and candied citrus strips.

[serves 4]

Citrus Napoleon

Nothing says fancy like a layered dessert. In a rush? Substitute lemon pudding or canned lemon curd for lemon cream and purchased whipped cream for home-made.

Preheat oven to 200°C/Gas Mark 6. In a small saucepan, combine sugar, water, lemon juice and cinnamon sticks. Bring to the boil, and reduce to a simmer for about 25 to 30 minutes until a thick syrup is achieved. Add honey and continue to cook for an additional 10 minutes. Remove from heat and allow to cool while assembling pastry.

Brush the bottom and sides of a 25 × 30-cm dish with melted butter. Filo dough will dry out easily. Have a damp tea towel available to keep dough covered and moist between usage.

Begin layering by placing six or seven sheets of filo pastry into the dish, brushing each thoroughly with butter before adding another sheet. Top the seventh filo sheet with ground nuts. Top the nut layer with two additional filo sheets, brushing each thoroughly with butter before adding another. Repeat the layering with nuts after every two sheets of filo; repeat until five or six layers of nuts have been used, brushing each layer with butter.

Top with the remaining seven or eight sheets of filo, buttering each one individually. Using a very sharp knife, measure the Baklava and cut it into diamond-shaped pieces. Do not cut all the way through the pastry, only halfway through it.

Brush the top with butter. Place in preheated oven. Reduce the temperature immediately to 190°C/Gas Mark 5, and bake for 10 to 12 minutes. Lower the oven to 180°C/Gas Mark 4 and bake for an additional 30 to 40 minutes or until golden brown. Remove from the oven and cool for 10 minutes. Pour cool syrup over hot Baklava. Let set for several hours before cutting pastry, so syrup will drain through to the bottom.

Let it set overnight before serving. Do not cover airtight.

450g filo pastry

450g butter, clarified

225g pecans, ground

225g walnuts, ground

FOR SYRUP:

700g sugar

500ml water

Juice from half of a fresh lemon

2 cinnamon sticks

3 Tbsp honey

[makes about 3 dozen diamond-shaped pieces]

Traditional Baklava

It seemed my Mother laboured for hours over the many layers of filo, butter and nuts in this dish, but the end result was always worth it. Today, I realise it doesn't take much time at all to make such a rich dessert.

A variation on the classic, this tiramisu has the rich flavours of coffee and Marsala wine and the subtle texture of the ladyfingers. Layered with a creamy filling, your guests will be delighted at the flavours, and you will be delighted with the ease of preparing it.

[serves 6]

Classic Tiramisu

To make the syrup, in a bowl stir together 225g sugar, boiling water, coffee, and the rum until the sugar is dissolved. Set aside. For the filling, beat the egg yolks and icing sugar together with an electric mixer until pale and thick. Slowly beat in 1 tablespoon of the liqueur and the Marsala. Add the mascarpone cheese, and beat until the mixture is thick and smooth. Add the egg whites, folding to incorporate. Soak the ladyfingers in the syrup. Drop three ladyfinger pieces in the bottom of each of six wine glasses. Spoon in half the mascarpone, and sprinkle with half the grated chocolate. Repeat the layers with the remaining soaked ladyfingers, mascarpone and chocolate. Cover and chill glasses for at least 2 hours. Before serving, top with whipped cream and toasted hazelnuts.

12 ladyfingers, broken into thirds

FOR SYRUP:

100g sugar

100ml boiling water

50ml strong brewed coffee (espresso is best)

50ml dark rum

FOR FILLING:

3 egg yolks, reserving egg whites

2 Tbsp icing sugar

2 Tbsp orange-flavoured liqueur

1 Tbsp sweet Marsala

225g mascarpone cheese

3 egg whites, beaten until fluffy and stiff peaks form

TOPPING:

two 30g squares dark chocolate, grated

whipped cream

30g toasted, chopped hazelnuts

1kg ripe strawberries, hulled and thinly sliced

225ml light red wine, such as Charbono or Chianti

100g plus 2 Tbsp sugar

30g cup finely chopped walnuts

30g cup finely chopped pecans

2 Tbsp cinnamon

2 Tbsp sugar

1/2 tsp nutmeg, freshly ground

10 sheets of filo pastry dough, thawed and kept moist

225g unsalted butter, clarified

8 large egg yolks

Finely grated zest of 1 orange

75ml Moscato or other sparkling wine

Large bunch of mint

Make-Ahead Ideas

Make the strawberries well in advance to ensure proper maceration of the juices. The filo crisps can be made a few days ahead and kept sealed in an airtight container. The zabaglione should be made fresh before serving.

Preheat the oven to 190°C/Gas Mark 5. In a medium-sized bowl, macerate the strawberries with the red wine and 2 tablespoons sugar for up to 2 hours, stirring from time to time to dissolve the sugar.

In a small bowl, combine the nuts and set aside. In another small bowl, combine the cinnamon, sugar and nutmeg, and set aside.

On a large, clean, flat work surface, unwrap and unroll the filo dough, being careful not to tear it. Dampen a tea towel with water to have on hand to keep the unused filo dough moist. Whenever the stack of filo dough is not being used, make sure to cover it with the dampened towel, because the dough will quickly dry out and become brittle and unusable. Using the clarified butter, coat a 25 × 30-cm Swiss roll tray thoroughly. Working in stages, separate one sheet of filo from the package, and place it flat on the buttered tray. Brush lightly but thoroughly with clarified butter. Sprinkle with a dusting of the spice mixture. Repeat this process with five sheets of filo, buttering thoroughly between every sheet and sprinkling every sheet with spices. After the fifth layer of filo dough is coated with butter, sprinkle the nut mixture evenly over. Continue again with the layers of the remaining filo dough, buttering and dusting with spices after every one. Make sure that the last filo sheet is covered thoroughly with butter and again dusted with spices. With a very sharp knife, gently score the filo dough so that it forms eight even squares. Only cut through the nut layer at this stage. Bake the filo sheets on the centre shelf until golden brown and crisp, about 20 minutes. Remove from the oven and let cool. Once they are cool, cut through to the bottom of the slices that you already created, ensuring that the filo is separated into eight equal parts. Set aside until assembling the dessert.

Put the egg yolks in a large, heatproof bowl, add the remaining 100g sugar and whisk until light and fluffy. Bring a large pot of water to the boil over high heat. Whisk the orange zest and Moscato into the egg yolks. Put the bowl on top of the pot of boiling water, and whisk until the zabaglione is fluffy, stiff and pale yellow, about 5 minutes.

[To assemble]

Place a filo square in the centre of a dessert plate. Add a layer of strawberries, ensuring that the juice is running down on to the plate, then a scoop of zabaglione. Top with the remaining layer of filo, add another layer of strawberries and top with a dollop of zabaglione. Garnish with a sprig of mint and serve.

[serves 8]

Spiced Filo with Strawberries and Zabaglione

Layers of crisp filo squares and sparkling sweet strawberries couple with creamy zabaglione in this elegant and simple dessert, but any fruit can be used to create dramatic layers. When in season, strawberries are perfect with the champagne zabaglione.

Cook pasta sheets according to package directions, cool and dry thoroughly. Combine the cinnamon and sugar in a small bowl. Once the pasta is dry, cut each sheet into thirds lengthways.

Pour oil for frying into a heavy-bottomed saucepan, and heat on medium to high heat. Add pasta sheets in batches of two. They will appear to stick to the bottom of the pan. Do not attempt to scrape them loose. They should float to the top of the pot shortly after dropping in. If one persists in sticking to the pot, gently scrape or push it from underneath with a Teflon-coated spatula. Fry the pasta until golden, about $1^1/2$ to 2 minutes on each side. Remove and place them on kitchen paper. Sprinkle both sides of the pasta with the cinnamon-sugar mixture.

[For candied nuts]
Melt butter in a small frying pan over medium heat. Add the chopped nuts and stir to coat with butter. Cook for about 5 minutes to toast, stirring constantly. Add sugar, brown sugar, cinnamon, nutmeg and a pinch of salt. Combine and cook for an additional 3 minutes until the sugar is melted. Remove from heat and spread in a single layer on foil or greaseproof paper to cool.

[To make chocolate ganache]
Place the grated chocolate in a small bowl. In a small saucepan, heat the double cream just until bubbly around the edges, about 4 minutes. Pour the warmed heavy cream over the chocolate and stir until the chocolate melts. Add the butter and continue to stir until well combined. Set aside until assembly.

[For the Crème Anglaise]
In a small saucepan, scald the milk. Heat until the milk is just bubbling along the sides of the pan and steam is rising from the milk, about 4 minutes.

While the milk is heating, in a small mixing bowl, combine the eggs and sugar. Whisk them together until the mixture is smooth and pale yellow. Add about 50ml of warm milk to the egg mixture, and whisk until combined. This is to temper the eggs to ensure that they don't scramble when added to the milk. Add the egg and sugar mixture to the milk, stirring constantly. Cook on low heat until the mixture has thickened slightly and coats the back of a metal spoon. (Do not allow it to boil, or the sauce will curdle.) Remove the pan from the heat and set aside.

[To assemble]
Paint each crispy noodle on one side with the chocolate. On a dessert plate, spoon crème Anglaise in a circular fashion to "paint" the plate. Place one crispy pasta sheet on the plate, chocolate-side up. Top with a scoop of softened vanilla ice cream. Place another crispy pasta sheet chocolate-side up on top of the ice cream. Spoon additional crème Anglaise on the top and sprinkle with candied nuts. Garnish with a mint leaf and dust plate with cocoa.

[serves 6]

Fried Pasta with Chocolate Ganache and Ice Cream

Fried pasta? You will love this dish. The crisp, biscuity texture of the pasta, brushed with chocolate, is the perfect accompaniment to your favourite ice cream.

4 previously cooked pasta sheets, cut into thirds

1 Tbsp ground cinnamon

1 Tbsp sugar

corn or vegetable oil for frying

FOR CANDIED NUTS:

2 Tbsp unsalted butter

15g chopped pecans

15g chopped walnuts

1 tsp sugar

2 Tbsp brown sugar

½ tsp cinnamon

¼ tsp nutmeg

salt

FOR CHOCOLATE GANACHE:

100g dark chocolate, grated

50ml double cream

1 Tbsp butter

FOR CRÈME ANGLAISE:

225ml milk

3 egg yolks

30g sugar

50ml warm milk

vanilla ice cream

mint leaves and cocoa for garnish

FOR THE PASTRY:

115g plus 1 Tbsp plain flour

50g crumbled gingersnaps

1 tsp ground cinnamon

pinch of salt

8 Tbsp unsalted butter, at room temperature

2 large egg yolks, at room temperature

100g sugar

FOR THE PASTRY CREAM:

500ml milk

6 large egg yolks, at room temperature

170g sugar

6 Tbsp plain flour

generous pinch of salt

1 tsp vanilla extract

FOR THE FILLING:

350g best-quality ricotta

100g sugar

1 large egg yolk, at room temperature

zest of 2 lemons, grated

1/2 tsp lemon extract

zest of 1 orange, grated

In a wide mixing bowl, use a whisk to combine the flour, crumbled gingersnaps, cinnamon, and salt. Shape into a mound, forming a well in the centre. Place the butter, egg yolks, and sugar in the well, mixing the contents of the well only to combine. (Using your fingers is generally the most effective way to do this.) Gradually work in the flour from the sides with your fingers (a fork can be effective as well). The mixture will become crumbly and feel as if it is coming together, and at this time use the heel of your hand to push it gently down and away from you, smearing it across the bowl. This will blend all the ingredients. When the dough holds together, pat it into a small disc, cover it and let it stand for 30 minutes, allowing the gluten to relax.

Preheat the oven to 180°C/Gas Mark 4. On a clean, dry work surface, roll the dough to 3mm thick. The dough will be used to cover the bottom and sides of a 23-cm springform cake tin. Cut a disk out of the dough using the bottom of the tin as a guide. Fit the dough into the bottom of the tin. For the sides, simply cut the remainder of the dough into strips only so long that they are easy to handle. Wrap these strips around the sides of the tin, coming up about 5cm from the bottom. Using your fingers, press all seams of the dough together, making sure that there is a consistent thickness throughout. Bake the dough, unlined and covered until it is pale golden but not cooked through, about 15 minutes. Let it cool.

[For pastry cream]
Scald 400ml milk in a medium-sized heavy saucepan over medium heat. Remove from the heat, cover, and let sit for 10 minutes.

In the bowl of a food processor, whisk the egg yolks and sugar together until they are thick and pale yellow and a ribbon forms when you lift the whisk from the bowl, about 5 minutes. Add the flour and salt and continue to whisk until blended, then add the reserved 50ml of milk. Whisk the hot milk into the egg mixture, and add the vanilla. Pour the mixture back into the saucepan. Bring it to the boil for 2 minutes over medium-high heat, whisking constantly. Remove it from the heat and immediately transfer the pastry cream to a bowl to cool slightly.

[For the filling]
In the bowl of a food processor fitted with the blade attachment, mix the ricotta, sugar, egg yolk, lemon and orange zest until blended. Add the cooled pastry cream, and mix until thoroughly combined. Pour the mixture over the prebaked crust.

Bake the torte in the centre of the oven until the top is golden and a knife inserted into the centre comes out clean, about 70 minutes. Remove the torte from the oven, and cool it on a wire rack for 10 minutes. Remove the sides of the tin and continue to cool it completely before serving.

[serves 12]

Citrus Ricotta Torte

While not a layered dessert, I thought it was fitting to add this recipe to the book because of its use of ricotta. The gingersnaps in the crust give a bite to the flavours, accentuating the citrus in the filling. Serve the cake chilled with an espresso.

chapter 7

A Few Key Recipes

Béchamel Sauce

[yields 1 litre]

Béchamel, or *besciamella,* is a basic staple of northern Italian cooking.

800ml full cream milk

7 Tbsp unsalted butter

7 Tbsp plain flour

salt

Scald the milk in a medium-sized saucepan (look for small bubbles forming around the edge) over low heat for about 4 minutes. Remove it from the heat but keep it warm. In another medium-sized saucepan, melt the butter over medium heat until completely melted. Whisk in the flour and let the mixture foam and cook, whisking occasionally, for 3 minutes or until it is a light tan colour (you will notice a nutty aroma to the mixture). Slowly whisk in the hot milk and cook, whisking regularly, until the sauce thickens, about 5 minutes. If the milk has cooled, add it gradually in small portions, whisking between each addition to prevent lumps. If the sauce isn't thickening, increase the heat slightly and whisk constantly so as not to burn it. Season the béchamel sauce with salt to taste and remove from the heat. Cool before using in lasagne dishes.

For added flavour, not necessarily suited for all dishes, stud one peeled medium onion with four whole cloves and place in the milk during the heating process. Remove the onion before adding the milk to the flour and butter mixture.

Bolognese Meat Sauce

[yields 1 litre]

This hearty meat sauce is probably the most traditional—with the exception of tomato sauce—in Italian cooking.

2 Tbsp olive oil

1 Tbsp butter

150g minced beef

150g minced pork

150g minced veal

75g prosciutto, finely chopped

1 large onion, chopped

1 medium carrot, peeled and chopped

2 stalks celery, cleaned and chopped

3 garlic cloves, crushed

2 sprigs Italian parsley, finely chopped

1 bay leaf, crumbled

1/2 tsp fresh rosemary, finely chopped

225ml beef stock

1 medium ripe tomato, peeled, seeded and chopped

225g fresh mushrooms, sliced

225ml dry red wine

225ml milk

1/4 tsp nutmeg

In a large stockpot, heat the olive oil and melt the butter. Brown the beef, pork, veal and prosciutto. Add the onion, carrot, celery, garlic, parsley, bay leaf and rosemary, and cook on medium heat for 10 minutes. Add the beef stock and tomatoes. Cook for 5 minutes. Add the mushrooms and cook for an additional 5 minutes. Increase the heat to medium-high, add the red wine and cook for 2 minutes until the smell of wine subsides. Add milk and nutmeg, and reduce heat to a gentle simmer. Simmer uncovered for 1 1/2 to 2 hours until thick and hearty, stirring occasionally.

4 red peppers or 450g jar of roasted red peppers, drained

2 Tbsp extra-virgin olive oil

500ml double cream

75g freshly grated Parmesan cheese

1/8 tsp salt

1/2 tsp black pepper

2 cloves garlic, crushed

2 Tbsp fresh chopped basil leaves or 1 Tbsp dried

[yields approximately 750ml]

Fire-Roasted Red Pepper Sauce

[Roasting the peppers]
Wash and dry the peppers thoroughly. On a large platter, coat the red peppers with 2 tablespoons of olive oil. On a hot grill, under the grill of a gas or electric cooker or over an open flame on a gas cooker top, roast the peppers until the skin is charred black, turning them occasionally to ensure even roasting. When completely charred, place the peppers in a brown paper bag, sealing it shut for about 5 minutes. This technique will make it easier to remove the burned skin. Remove the peppers from the bag and remove the black skin, revealing the velvety, vibrant red flesh. Cut the peppers in half and remove the stems, seeds and inner white veins. Chop the peppers coarsely and set them aside.

[Preparing the sauce]
In a heavy, medium-sized saucepan, heat the double cream. Add the grated Parmesan cheese, salt and pepper to the cream and continue to heat it, stirring occasionally, until the cheese is melted and the sauce thickens. In the bowl of a food processor, combine the roasted red peppers and garlic. Process the mixture until you have a purée. Add the pepper purée to the double cream mixture and combine. Heat through. Add the basil and stir. Remove from the heat and set aside until ready to use.

The sauce may be made ahead and stored in a refrigerated airtight container for up to three days. During autumn months, red peppers are in ample supply, with great quality and good prices. Roast the peppers any time and freeze them for later use. Make plenty of Fire-Roasted Red Pepper Sauce, package it and freeze it for up to three months.

Roasted red peppers are a tremendous addition to any dish. Their robust flavours and silky texture add such characteristic tastes. For this sauce, either home-roasted or bottled roasted red peppers are fine. But if time and patience permits, I suggest the home method over purchased. You won't be sorry when the end product is served.

Tips on Roasting Red Peppers

I have found that the easiest way to roast red peppers is on a gas grill. Turn the grill on high and roast the peppers until the skin is charred black, turning them periodically to ensure even roasting. If a grill is not readily available, the next best way to roast them (but a bit more dangerous and tedious) is on the open flame of a gas cooker. Just turn the burner on high. Use a carving fork to pierce the stem end of the pepper, hold it, and roast over the flame until the skin is charred black, turning it continuously to ensure even roasting. Be careful in selecting the fork to use. If the handle is heat resistant, then you are fine; if not or if you are not sure, use an oven glove so as not to burn your hands. As always be careful of the open flame, too. Make sure there are no animals or children around. If you have an electric stove, try the under-the-grill method, which works fine, but is just a bit more messy and smoky. Turn on the grill and place the oiled peppers in a roasting tin on the middle shelf of the oven. Let them grill, charring the skin black, turning them occasionally to ensure even roasting. While this method actually sounds like the easiest (which it probably is), it doesn't yield the same effect and robust flavour of an open flame, thus the name "fire-roasted." The smokiness of fire and the sweetness of the peppers is a perfect marriage.

[yields 1 litre]

Quick Tomato Sauce

Quick and powerful, this tomato sauce takes little prep time (you don't even chop the basil) and little cooking time. The trick is fresh basil. While many recipes can handle dried as a replacement for fresh, I do not recommend it in this case. This sauce is simply too good with the fresh basil.

1½ kg canned best-quality, peeled plum tomatoes with juice

4 cloves garlic, peeled and coarsely chopped

1 Tbsp coarse salt

1 Tbsp sugar

6 Tbsp extra-virgin olive oil

50g loosely packed fresh basil leaves

2 Tbsp tomato purée

¼ tsp black pepper

2 tsp dried oregano

50ml cup red wine

Place all the ingredients in a large saucepan. Bring to the boil, stirring and boiling for about 5 minutes, crushing the tomatoes with the back of a spoon while stirring. Reduce the heat and simmer for 20 minutes, stirring occasionally. Serve immediately or refrigerate for up to five days. The sauce may be made, chilled and frozen in airtight containers for up to three months.

FOR THE PROCESSOR:

100g tightly packed fresh basil leaves

50g pine kernels

4 garlic cloves, chopped finely before putting in the processor

salt

100ml extra-virgin olive oil

FOR COMPLETION BY HAND:

75g freshly grated Parmigiano-Reggiano cheese

2 Tbsp Romano cheese, freshly grated

3 Tbsp butter, softened to room temperature

[yields 1 litre]

Basic Basil Pesto

Briefly soak and wash the basil in cold water, and gently pat it thoroughly dry with kitchen paper.

Place the basil, pine kernels, chopped garlic and an ample pinch of salt in the processor bowl and process for a few seconds. Add the olive oil, scrape the sides of the bowl, and continue to process the mixture until a uniform creamy consistency is achieved. Transfer the mixture to a bowl and mix in the Parmigiano-Reggiano and Romano cheeses by hand. It is worth the slight effort to do it by hand to obtain the notably superior texture it produces. When the cheese has been evenly amalgamated with the other ingredients, mix in the softened butter, distributing it uniformly into the sauce. When spooning the pesto over pasta, dilute it slightly with a tablespoon or two of the hot water in which the pasta was cooked.

A Note on Cheese

Classical pesto is made with the Pecorino cheese known as Fiore Sardo. It is a less harsh flavour than that of Romano. Romano, however, is readily available. With this recipe, the proportion of Romano to Parmigiano-Reggiano is less than what you will want to use if you can get Fiore Sardo. If you are able to find Fiore Sardo use 75g Fiore Sardo to 2 tablespoons of grated Parmigiano-Reggiano.

Freezing Pesto

Make the pesto in the food processor, freezing it without the cheese and butter. Add the cheese and butter when it is thawed, just before using. Pesto may be frozen in an airtight container for several months. Summer is the best time of year for the freshest basil. Make yourself several batches of pesto and freeze them for when fresh, good-quality basil is not available.

Basil pesto, with its vibrant green colour and tremendous flavour, is another Italian staple. It is as rich in history as it is in taste. Italian culinary traditions suggest that there is no other way to make pesto but by the mortar and pestle method, yet the nearly effortless food processor method given here is a fine substitute.

The long cooking time of this sauce establishes intense, concentrated flavours. Use this in place of the quick sauce in any of the dishes in this book or simply to top spaghetti.

[yields 500 ml]

Slow-Simmered Tomato Sauce

100ml olive oil

1 medium onion, finely chopped

1 large carrot, peeled and finely chopped

50g fresh mushrooms, sliced

4 garlic cloves, crushed

700g ripe tomatoes, peeled

170ml dry white or red wine

1 Tbsp fresh oregano, finely chopped

1 Tbsp fresh basil, chopped

1/2 tsp fresh thyme, finely chopped

2 tsp sugar

2 Tbsp freshly grated Parmesan cheese

salt and freshly ground black pepper to taste

In a small frying pan, heat 4 tablespoons of the olive oil, and sauté the onion and carrot until translucent, about 8 minutes. Add the mushrooms and garlic, and continue to sauté until tender. Remove from the heat and set aside. Heat the remaining olive oil in a heavy, medium-sized saucepan, and add the tomatoes. Simmer over low heat, breaking up the tomatoes with a wooden spoon, about 10 minutes. Add the onion, mushrooms, wine, garlic, oregano, basil, thyme, sugar and cheese, cover, and simmer very gently for 2 1/2 to 3 hours. Season with salt and pepper.

Making Fresh Pasta Dough

Making fresh pasta dough is simple. There are some basic techniques to consider when making the dough, but nothing that relies on any amount of culinary expertise. I have included two methods for making the fresh dough: by hand and by food processor.

Now, I would be remiss in not saying that the "by hand" method is the classically preferred way to make truly great fresh pasta dough. The gradual process of hand-kneading the dough, coupled with the warmth from your hands, creates a far superior texture to the dough than a machine can make. However, in the interests of time and appropriate worktop space in today's kitchens, the food processor method results in a great dough as well.

Fresh Pasta—By Hand Method

The amount of the flour is an approximate measurement due to the variable moisture in eggs, as well as the variation in humidity in your kitchen. You can adjust the amount before you begin to knead the dough.

250g plain flour

3 large eggs, at room temperature

Pour the flour into a mound on a wooden or other smooth, warm work surface. (Stone or marble countertops are not a good surface for this because of their cold temperature.) Using your hand, make a well in the centre of the flour mound. Crack the eggs one at a time into the well. Beat the eggs gently with a fork until the whites and yolks are evenly combined. Using the fork, begin to incorporate the flour gradually from the sides of the well into the eggs, stirring until the eggs are no longer runny. Be careful not to break the sides of the well because the eggs will run.

At this point, work quickly to incorporate the remainder of the flour with the egg. Using both hands, bring the remaining flour over the egg mixture, covering it completely. Work the dough with your hands until all the flour is combined with the eggs. This is where more flour may be needed. The dough should be moist, but not sticky. When it feels the right consistency, remove it from the work surface and wrap it up. Clean your work surface of all debris. Wash your hands to remove any egg or flour. Dry the work surface and your hands. Unwrap the dough and return it to the work surface. Begin kneading. Hold the dough with one hand, while folding it over with the other. Use the heel of your palm to push the dough down and away from you, continuing to fold it over. Rotate the dough a quarter turn during this two-part process of folding and pushing. Continue this kneading process until the dough is uniform and very smooth. Wrap it immediately in clingfilm and let it rest for at least 20 minutes before rolling it out.

For Coloured Pasta

Spinach pasta (green)

350g fresh spinach, cleaned, or 200g frozen spinach

[For fresh spinach]
In boiling, salted water, cook the spinach until tender, about 2 minutes. Remove it from the water, drain it, and squeeze it dry. Finely chop it before using.

[For frozen spinach]
Simply thaw and drain it, squeezing out any excess water. Finely chop it before using. Add the spinach to the beaten eggs, and incorporate it thoroughly before adding the flour. From this point, follow all the steps for making the fresh dough. More flour will probably be needed because of the added moisture from the spinach.

Tomato pasta (red)

3 Tbsp tomato purée

Add the tomato purée to the beaten eggs, and incorporate it thoroughly before adding the flour. From this point, follow all the steps for making the fresh dough. More flour may be needed; adjust this prior to the kneading step.

Food Processor Method

300g plain flour	
50g cake flour	
5 eggs, at room temperature	
1 Tbsp extra-virgin olive oil	

Place both flours in the bowl of a food processor fitted with the blade attachment. Pulse the flour to combine it. Beat the eggs together with the olive oil in a small bowl. With the processor running, add the egg-oil mixture to the flour. When the dough forms a ball, stop the processor. Remove the dough from the bowl, and place it on a clean, dry, warm work surface.

Begin to knead the dough, dusting it with a little flour to make it easier to handle. Follow the kneading techniques for the "by-hand" method. Wrap the dough and let it rest for at least 20 minutes before rolling it out. For flavoured or coloured dough, add the spinach or tomato purée into the bowl with the egg and oil, using the same measurements as for the by-hand dough. The flour is an approximate measurement; more may need to be added. Adjust the flour prior to kneading.

Rolling the Dough

There are two techniques for rolling dough: by machine and by hand. Rolling by hand is done with a rolling pin. A long pin with no handles, similar to a wooden dowel, is preferred. While this technique is more labour-intensive and time-consuming, the result is a much more porous dough with a smooth texture, which will absorb sauces better.

[Rolling by hand]

Begin by unwrapping the dough and placing it on a clean, flat, warm work surface. Knead the dough for a couple of minutes to incorporate any moisture that may have gathered on top of the dough. Flatten the dough a little with your hands to make a round disk. Begin rolling with the pin from the middle of the disc, working outwards to just before the edge of the disc. Rotate the dough ninety degrees and repeat the rolling. Continue this rolling until the dough is about 5mm thick. Repeat the process five times. This process is stretching the dough instead of rolling and flattening it. Continue to stretch it until it becomes transparent. Lay the dough on a tea towel in a warm, dry place to dry. When ready to use, simply cut the dough into rectangular sheets.

[Rolling by machine]

The pasta must be stretched and thinned out gradually. Pasta machines are equipped with an adjustable gauge that dictates the width between the rollers, allowing for gradual thinning.

Uncover the dough and knead to incorporate moisture that may have collected while resting. Cut the dough into six equal pieces. Working with one piece at a time and being sure to cover the unused pieces, knead the dough into a flat rectangle that will fit through the rolling machine. Set the rollers at the widest setting and begin passing the dough through. Pick up the dough as it comes through, being careful not to stretch it or pull it. Fold the dough in thirds. Turn it so that the folds are at the sides, and pass it through the machine again. Repeat this folding and rolling process three or four times until the dough is very smooth. Repeat with the other pieces of dough. Reduce the width of the machine by one notch. Pass all the pieces of dough through the roller once, laying them out on tea towels. Reduce the roller width another notch. Continue rolling all the pieces of dough on each width setting until they have each passed through the machine at the thinnest setting. Cut the pasta to desired size and set aside, covered, until ready to use.

Index

Acknowledgements

A cookbook is always a collaboration, a collection of thoughts, ideas, and contributions inspired by many family, friends, and colleagues. This book is no exception. For their many talents, skillful guidance, and creative graphic design, I wish to thank my editor Donna Raskin and art director Silke Braun, as well as Tim and Liz Prescott for their artful eye with food styling and Ron Manville, photographer and friend. A recipe doesn't become a published recipe without the discriminating and critical tastes of those chosen as recipe testers and tasters. Having a close circle of friends and family comes in very handy with this grueling task. I would like to thank Randy Mills, Steve and Erin Sears, Cliff and Kathy McGovern, Kerry and Brian Parent, and Richard Carbotti for their appreciation of good food and their unbridled approach to critiquing my food.

Thanks also to Tony Montefusco, the best friend and support a guy could ever wish for. Many thanks and much gratitude to Hans Stahl, for without his vision and confidence in me, this book would not be a reality. As you go along through life, there will always be those people you meet and befriend that will have some relevant impact on your present and future. To Martha Murphy, I thank you for your inspiration and friendship over the years. To my Camp Mystic friends and family—Dick and Tweety Eastland, Anne Eastland Spears, and Phillip and Jeanne Stacey— you gave me the opportunity and springboard from which I expanded my mind and talents in the kitchen; thank you. And of course a world of thanks goes to my family for their endless support and encouragement with whatever I do.

Lastly, thank you to all the readers who indulge in the pages of this book. Enjoy!

Lasagne

Over 50 Recipes for
Everyone's Favourite Dish

Lasagne

Dwayne Ridgaway

APPLE

Packaged Goods
33 Commercial Street
Gloucester, MA 01930
(978) 282-9590

Photography by Ron Manville, with the exception of: Michael Paul Photography:
page 116

ISBN 1-84092-412-8

10 9 8 7 6 5 4 3 2 1

Printed in China.

Editorial Director:
Donna Raskin

**Creative and
Photo Direction:**
Silke Braun

Art Direction:
Claire MacMaster

Managing Editor:
Wendy Simard

Photo Editor:
Jennifer Beal

Design:
Wilson Harvey,
London

Photography:
Ron Manville

Food styling:
Tim and Elizabeth
Prescott

For my mother and grandmothers, for without them and the
love that their kitchens exude, this book would not be a reality.

Contents

Layer upon Layer
of History

Lasagne belongs to a family of baked pasta dishes known in Italy as *pasticci,* or twice-cooked pasta. For pasticci, the pasta is boiled, mixed, or layered with prepared ingredients or sauces, then baked.

Almost any pasta shape can be used for pasticci, but lasagne is most likely the original one used for baked dishes. For that matter, lasagne is probably the oldest known type of pasta. It's certainly the easiest to make. After rolling out pasta dough, you're left with a flat, wide sheet—the dictionary definition of "lasagne." But the meaning of lasagne goes deeper than that. Of course, the term "lasagne" refers to the popular casserole that features the pasta. But even deeper, many word historians believe that "lasagne" originally referred to the cooking vessel itself.

Given this word's etymology, it makes sense that "lasagne" now refers to both the pasta and the dish. Sometimes the definition gets stretched even further to include any baked casserole that is layered in a manner similar to traditional lasagne. For instance, some versions of courgette lasagne layer wide strips of courgette among sauces and cheeses, omitting the pasta altogether. I've even read a book on "lasagne gardening," an agricultural method that relies on the principle of layering inherent in the classic Italian dish. This makes for three key elements in the definition of "lasagne": (1) wide, flat sheets, (2) layers, and (3) a cooking vessel in which the dish is both cooked and served.

In keeping with the more liberal definition of lasagne, the recipes in this book employ at least two, if not all three, of lasagne's key elements. For example, I've included a few Italian layered desserts such as tiramisu and tortes. These dishes don't feature pasta, but they are layered and served in the dish in which they are prepared. You'll also find a lasagne gratin, which uses lasagne sheets and a lasagne dish but dispenses with the time-consuming layering. A few other recipes, such as fresh apple lasagne and Mexican tortilla lasagne, take creative licence with the idea of this classic dish. The rest of the book is devoted to variations on the traditional theme of boiled lasagne layered with various cheeses, sauces and fillings, then cooked and served in the same dish.

Lasagne-**Making Basics**